workbook
Innovations

a course in natural English

Hugh Dellar and Andrew Walkley

HEINLE
CENGAGE Learning

Australia • Brazil • Japan • Korea • Mexico • Singapore • Spain • United Kingdom • United States

Innovations Pre-Intermediate Workbook:
Dellar / Walkey

Publisher: Christopher Wenger

Series Editor: Jimmie Hill

Director of Development: Anita Raducanu

Director of Marketing: Amy Mabley

Editorial Manager: Howard Middle / HM ELT Services

Intl.Marketing Manager: Eric Bredenberg

Editor: Liz Driscoll

Production Management: Process ELT (www.process-elt.com)

Sr.Print Buyer: Mary Beth Hennebury

Associate Marketing Manager:Laura Needham

Illustrator: Nick Dimitriadis

Photo Researcher: Process ELT

Cover/Text Designer: Studio Image & Photo-graphic Art (www.studio-image.com)

Printer: Seng Lee Press

Photo Credits

Page 8 © Mark Cass/Brand X Pictures/PictureQuest;page 12 © Rich Remsberg/Index Stock Imagery;page 15 © Creatas/PictureQuest;page 21 © DigitalVision/PictureQuest; page 33 © DigitalVision/PictureQuest;page 37 © DigitalVision/PictureQuest;page 38 (top) © Creatas/PictureQuest;page 38 (middle) © SW Produc-tions/ Brand X Pictures/PictureQuest;page 38 (bottom) © BananaStock/BananaStock,Ltd./PictureQuest;page 44 © Cary Wolinsky/Stock,Boston Inc./PictureQuest;page 53 © Associated Press/John d McHugh;page 57 © Painet Inc.;page 62 © Corbis Images/PictureQuest;page 64 © Associated Press/Kevork Djansezian;page 70 © DigitalVision/PictureQuest;page 71 © Florian Frank/Brand X Pictures/PictureQuest;page 83 © Crea-tas/PictureQuest;page 87 © Image Ideas, Inc./PictureQuest

ISBN 10: 0-7593-9621-3

ISBN 13: 978-0-7593-9621-0

Heinle
High Holborn House, 50-51 Bedford Row
London WC1R 4LR

Cengage Learning is a leading provider of customised learning solutions with office locations around the globe, including Singapore, the United Kingdom, Australia, Mexico, Brazil and Japan. Locate our local office at: **international.cengage.com/region**

Cengage Learning products are represented in Canada by Nelson Education, Ltd.

Visit Heinle online at **http://elt.heinle.com**
Visit our corporate website at www.**cengage.com**

Printed in Singapore
2 3 4 5 6 7 8 9 10 – 10 09 08

To the student

It's important to study outside class. Learning a language takes a long time, but it can happen a bit quicker if you study at home.

This Workbook includes a lot of the language you will study in class. It helps you to remember this language and to learn how to use it better. It gives you more opportunities to practise grammar, it helps you to check your understanding of how to use new vocabulary in typical, everyday situations and it helps you with your written English too.

Here is some advice on how to use the book.

- Do a little every day rather than a lot once a week.
- Try to do an exercise first without using the answer key, but use the answer key if you have a problem.
- If you still have any questions about the language in the book, ask your teacher.
- Look back at earlier units in the book after you have finished them. It is important to make sure you remember what you have already studied. Sometimes, just re-reading exercises you did a few weeks before can help you to remember things.
- Before you start working on your own, study the Introduction on page 7.

Contents

Introduction

The main goal of the INNOVATIONS series is to help you speak English fluently and understand spoken English. Because of this, most of the exercises in this book give spoken models of how the language is normally used. One of the most important things to think about when studying English on your own is collocation.

1 What is a collocation?

A collocation is two or more words which go together. This often means an adjective + a noun, a verb + a noun, or a noun + a noun. Some of the exercises in this book look at collocations of common words – *have, sort out, get* – because it is important to learn how to use these useful words in lots of different ways.

Match the verbs with the nouns to make collocations.

1. go ☐   a. tennis
2. play ☐   b. in a bank
3. send ☐   c. medicine
4. work ☐   d. swimming
5. study ☐   e. an e-mail

Now match these adjectives with the nouns to make collocations.

6. strong ☐   f. bag
7. a long ☐   g. fan of Bob Marley
8. a heavy ☐   h. coffee
9. a big ☐   i. subject to study
10. a useful ☐ j. way to walk

Learning new collocations is a big part of learning a language. You need to be careful when translating into your own language. It is always better to translate collocations – or even whole sentences – than single words.

2 Making the most of your self-study time

Translating from English into your own language is normal at this level. When you study this book at home, it is a good idea to also keep your own vocabulary notebook. Write down new bits of English on the left and translations on the right. Here is an exercise which shows you how to translate well.

Start your vocabulary notebook by copying the sentences below on a page. Write a translation next to each sentence in your own language. Test yourself in a week's time. Cover the sentences and use your translations to help you remember the whole sentences in English.

1. What're you doing tonight?
2. Have you been there?
3. It's the second city.
4. How long've you been doing that?
5. Not very long. Only about a month.
6. Did you have a nice weekend?
7. Let's go to the café round the corner.
8. I went to bed really late last night.

3 Grammatical terms

This Workbook gives you plenty of chances to look at the most common, useful grammatical structures in English. You will look at both how to form these structures and how to use them in everyday contexts.

Match the underlined words in the sentences with the grammatical terms.

1. I'm meeting a friend of mine later. ☐
2. I've never heard of it. ☐
3. That was the worst film I've ever seen. ☐
4. There's one in my bag. ☐
5. I just stayed at home. ☐
6. This one is better. ☐
7. I don't feel well. ☐
8. Sorry. I wasn't looking where I was going. ☐

a. a comparative adjective   e. past continuous
b. present continuous   f. past simple
c. present perfect simple   g. a preposition
d. a superlative adjective   h. an adverb

1 Where are you from?

1 Starting conversations

Match the conversation starters with the replies.

1. What's your name? ☐
2. Where are you from? ☐
3. Is this the bus stop for the centre of town? ☐
4. Is anyone sitting here? ☐

a. No, you need to go to that one over there, on the other side of the road.
b. Tsuyoshi, but just call me Yoshi for short.
c. Panama, in Central America.
d. Sorry, I'm saving it for a friend.

Now match these conversation starters with the replies.

5. It's so hot! ☐
6. Have you been waiting for a long time? ☐
7. Do you know anyone here? ☐
8. What a horrible day! ☐

e. Yes, a few people. I was in the same class as Joan and Ali last term.
f. I know. It's awful, isn't it?
g. I know. It's boiling.
h. No, I only just got here myself.

2 Conversation

Complete the conversation with ONE word in each space.

C: Do you (1) .... ?

D: No, thanks. I'm trying to (2) ....

C: Yes, I should too. I'm sorry, what's your name (3) .... ?

D: Danko. And yours?

C: Caroline. Hi, so where are you from, Danko?

D: Croatia.

C: Oh, yes? Whereabouts (4) .... ? Zagreb?

D: No, Split. It's on the (5) .... Do you know it?

C: I've heard of it, but I've never been there. There was a tennis player from there, wasn't there? What's his name?

D: Goran Ivanisevic.

C: Yes, that's the one. He was lovely.

D: Yes, well you should come to Split. There are lots of lovely people there. It's a beautiful city.

C: I'd (6) .... to go one day. So how long have you been here in Britain?

D: Almost six months now. I came here in September.

C: Right. When are you (7) .... back to Croatia?

D: In May. I've got to go back then.

C: Why? What do you do back (8) .... ?

D: Oh, I'm a student. I'm at university. I have to (9) .... some exams in June.

C: Oh right. What are you studying?

D: English language and culture. That's the main (10) .... I'm here.

C: Right, right. Well, you speak English very well.

D: Thanks. I hope so.

C: No, really.

Write a conversation between YOU and Caroline. For example:

C: Do you smoke?

Y: No, I don't thanks, but don't let me stop you.

3 *Where* and *whereabouts*

Complete the descriptions with the names of the places on the map.

1. .... is a town on the north-west coast of England.

2. .... is in the north-west of England, very close to the border with Scotland.

3. .... is an island off the north coast of Wales.

4. .... is a city in the middle of England.

5. .... is in the north of Scotland.

6. .... is in the south-east of England.

7. .... is a town in the west of England, close to the border with Wales.

8. .... is a town in the south-west of Scotland, close to the border with England.

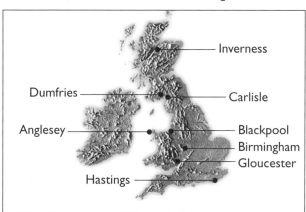

Inverness
Dumfries
Carlisle
Anglesey
Blackpool
Birmingham
Gloucester
Hastings

4 Whereabouts exactly is it?

Match the descriptions with the places on the map.

1. It's halfway down Lambert Street. ☐

2. It's on the right, just off Lambert Street. ☐

3. It's at this end of Lambert Street. ☐

4. It's at the end of Lambert Street. ☐

5. It's on the left, just past the mosque. ☐

6. It's just before you get to the mosque. ☐

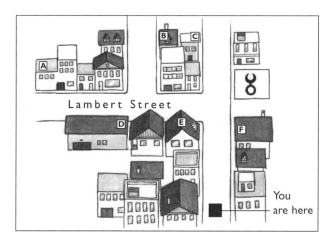

L a m b e r t S t r e e t

You are here

5 I'm not from here originally

Complete the paragraphs with the words in the boxes.

Paragraph 1

degree	escape	refugee	support

I'm a (1) .... I come from Ethiopia originally and came over here to (2) .... the fighting in my country. Back home, I was an engineer, but because my (3) .... is from Addis Ababa University, it's not recognised here. I'm doing two jobs at the moment to try to (4) .... my wife and children – I drive taxis at night and then do a cleaning job in the mornings. It's really hard work.

Paragraph 2

brought up	degree	unemployment
closed down	graduate	

I was born and (5) .... in Tomsk, a city in the centre of Russia. I moved to Moscow about six years ago because the factory I was working in (6) .... and I lost my job. There's a lot of (7) .... in my home town, so I decided to move to look for work. I've been working in a hotel for the last three years and I'm also doing a part-time (8) .... I finish next summer and I hope I can get a better job after I (9) ....

Paragraph 3

holiday	immigrant	miss	share

I'm an (10) .... here. I'm from Georgia originally and I came to London when I got married. My wife is English and we met when she was on (11) .... in Tblisi, my home town. I like it here most of the time, but I (12) .... the food and especially the wine from my country. I think Georgians are more relaxed and generous than people here. We (13) .... things more.

Language note: *share*

You can *share* lots of different things with other people – you can *share a flat* or *a room*. You can *share a taxi*, *share a pizza*, *share a book* and *share ideas*.

Translate *share* into your language. Can you use this word with all the things above?

6 Moving

Complete the sentences with the pairs of words in the box.

escape + safe	place + houses
family + old	sea + coast
get away from + know	study + university
job + unemployment	work + company

1. We moved to Berlin because of my mum's
    .... She works for a big
    multinational ....

2. I moved to Shanghai to look for a
    .... There was a lot of
    .... in my home town.

3. I left Sierra Leone to .... the war.
    It just wasn't .... there any more.

4. We moved to be nearer my wife's ....
    Her mum and dad are getting quite ....

5. We moved here so we could be by the ....
    We both grew up on the ....

6. I moved to Milan to .... There wasn't
    a .... in the place I lived in before.

7. I left Tel Aviv to .... my family. My
    mum always wanted to .... what
    I was doing all the time!

8. We moved out of the city because we needed a
    bigger .... It's a lot cheaper to buy
    .... down here.

7 There's / there are ...

Choose the correct form.

1. It's a great place to live. *There's / There are* lots of nice
    shops and cafés round there.

2. It's a bit boring sometimes. *There's / There are* not
    much to do round there.

3. It's quite a dangerous area. *There's / There are* quite a
    lot of crime round there.

4. I moved to the city because *there's / there are* quite
    high unemployment in my home town.

5. I moved to the city because *there's / there are* more
    jobs available here.

6. It's a great place to live. *There's / There are* a really
    good transport system, so it's very easy to get
    around.

7. It's quite a nice city, but *there's / there are* too many
    people living there. It's really crowded.

8. It's a very convenient place to live. *There's / There
    are* quite a few trains and buses that stop near
    there.

8 There's a ...

Complete the sentences with the words in the box.

bookshop	factory	supermarket
café	mall	take-away
cinema	park	

1. I don't cook very much. There's a really good
    Chinese .... near my house, so I
    usually just get something from there on the way
    home.

2. It's great where I live because there's a really nice
    .... near my house. I go jogging there
    and take my dog for a walk there in the mornings.

3. There's a really big shopping .... near
    my house. It's got everything – a McDonald's, a
    Starbucks, a Gap, a Levi's shop. It's great.

4. A: What're you reading? Oh, this looks interesting.
       Where did you get it?
    B: There's a French language .... near
       the station.

5. It's really bad where I live because there's a
    .... near my house and they work all
    night there. Sometimes it's so noisy, I can't sleep.

6. A: What're you doing now? Do you want to get
       something to eat?
    B: Yeah, I'd love to. There's a nice ....
       near here. We could get a sandwich and a drink
       there, if you want.

7. There's a really good .... near where I
    work. They're showing this French film tonight and it
    looks really good. Do you want to come and see it
    with me?

8. It's great where I live, because there's a
    .... near my house and it's open 24
    hours a day, so you can do your shopping at any
    time.

Complete each expression from the sentences above with ONE word.

a. on the .... home

b. .... my dog for a walk

c. I .... sleep

d. .... something to eat

e. near .... I work

f. it's .... 24 hours a day

9 *Miss* and *lose*

Complete the sentences with *miss, missed, lose* or *lost*.

1. I'm really worried about May. She's .... a lot of weight recently. Do you think she's OK?

2. I really .... going to the beach now I live in London. I lived by the sea when I was younger.

3. Did you see the match last night? Real Madrid .... 3–0 to Juventus.

4. Sorry I'm late. I got .... on the way here. I turned left coming out of the station, not right.

5. Sorry I .... class yesterday. I had to go to the dentist's.

6. Did you see that film last night? I .... the end because I had to go out. Do you know what happened?

7. Can you give me your address and phone number again? I've .... my address book.

8. Sorry I'm late. I woke up late and .... my bus.

9. My dad's working in Taipei at the moment. I really .... him.

10. Hurry up! I don't want to .... the beginning of the play.

10 Key words for writing: *so* and *because*

We use *so* to introduce the result and *because* to introduce the reason. For example:

- I didn't want to drive an hour a day to work, so we decided to move.

- We decided to move because I didn't want to drive an hour a day to work.

Complete the sentences with *so* or *because*.

1. It's quite boring here .... there's nothing to do.

2. There are lots of restaurants and cafés near my house, ... it's quite lively at night.

3. I live close to the school where I teach, ... I usually walk there. It's very convenient.

4. I usually take the train to work .... the traffic is really bad in my town.

5. I want to move house .... the place I live in now is too small.

11 Writing e-mails: changing address

Choose the correct words to complete this e-mail.

Dear Kathy

Sorry I haven't written to you recently, but I've been busy (1) .... a house. My husband got a new (2) .... in Kingston, which is more than one hour by car (3) .... where we live now. He didn't want to drive (4) .... , so we decided to move there. We (5) .... a very nice three-bedroom flat near a park. We've got (6) .... of space, so you must come and (7) .... with us. We're moving (8) .... Tuesday 13th. Our new address is: Flat 6, Sandringham Villas, 35 Queens Way, Kingston KS9 7BR. See you soon.
Love, Victoria

1. A looking for	B moving	C looking after	D trying
2. A work	B office	C company	D job
3. A of	B in	C from	D at
4. A every day	B all days	C all the days	D days
5. A find	B see	C saw	D found
6. A lots	B many	C much	D some
7. A visit	B stay	C live	D sleep
8. A on	B at	C in	D for

Read this e-mail from someone who is moving. Underline the common ways we start and finish e-mails. Then do the same for the e-mail above.

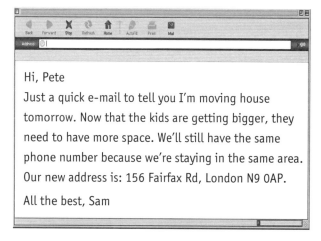

Hi, Pete
Just a quick e-mail to tell you I'm moving house tomorrow. Now that the kids are getting bigger, they need to have more space. We'll still have the same phone number because we're staying in the same area. Our new address is: 156 Fairfax Rd, London N9 0AP.
All the best, Sam

Write an e-mail to a friend about moving house. Tell them where you're moving to, why you're moving and what your new house and area are like. Invite them to visit. Use some of the language from this unit.

2 Likes and dislikes

1 Verb forms

Regular verbs have two basic forms. For example:

infinitive:	work	carry
past simple:	worked	carried
past participle:	worked	carried

However, many common verbs are irregular. For example:

infinitive:	do	put
past simple:	did	put
past participle:	done	put

Write the infinitive forms of these irregular verbs.

1. .... , went, gone
2. .... , took, taken
3. .... , broke, broken
4. .... , left, left
5. .... , read, read
6. .... , met, met
7. .... , chose, chosen
8. .... , ate, eaten
9. .... , forgot, forgotten
10. .... , fell, fallen
11. .... , knew, known
12. .... , drank, drunk
13. .... , saw, seen
14. .... , gave, given
15. .... , heard, heard
16. .... , bought, bought

2 Conversation

Complete the conversation with the words in the box.

ask	him	lend	same
else	it	lots	thinking
heard	kind	prefer	trying

K: Do you like opera?

J: No, I hate (1) .... I find it really boring. Why do you (2) .... ?

K: Oh, I'm (3) .... of going to see something at the Opera House and I'm (4) .... to find someone to go with.

J: No, sorry. I always think operas go on too long. I can't sit still for four hours.

K: Never mind. I'll try someone (5) ....

J: Have you asked Miriam? I think she likes that (6) .... of music.

K: Oh, right. OK. Maybe I'll ask her. So what kind of music do you like?

J: (7) .... of things, really. Jazz, pop, Latin music. I love Tito Lopez.

K: Really? I hate (8) .... All his songs sound the (9) .... I like jazz, though. Do you like Louis Armstrong?

J: Yes, he's OK. I quite like some of his tunes, but I (10) .... Gato Barbieri.

K: Oh right. I've never (11) .... of her. Who is she?

J: He's a man. He's an Argentinian musician. He's really good. I'll (12) .... you a CD, if you like.

K: Yes, OK. Thanks.

Can you remember where the pauses and the stressed sounds were in this conversation? Mark the pauses // and <u>underline</u> the stressed syllables. For example:

A: Do you like <u>o</u>pera?
B: No, I <u>hate</u> it. // I find it <u>real</u>ly <u>bor</u>ing. // <u>Why</u> do you <u>ask</u>?

Compare your ideas about the pauses and stressed sounds with the tapescript in the Coursebook.

3 Do you like … ?

Complete the conversations with the expressions in the box.

I've never heard of her.	They're OK, I suppose.
I've never heard of them.	Yes, I love him.
No, I hate it.	Yes, I love it.
No, not really.	Yes, it's OK.

1. A: Do you like action films?
   B: .... I prefer comedies.

2. A: Do you like swimming?
   B: .... I go swimming nearly every day. I hate the days when I can't go.

3. A: Do you like clubbing?
   B: .... I can't stand noisy places and I hate dancing.

4. A: Do you like watching football?
   B: .... I like watching the big games, but I don't really support any team.

5. A: Do you like Jackie Chan?
   B: .... I'm a really big fan of his.

6. A: Do you like Maria Carey?
   B: .... Who is she?

7. A: Do you like cooking?
   B: .... I often buy ready-made meals to put in the microwave.

8. A: Do you like The Screaming Trees?
   B: Who? .... What kind of music do they play?

4 What kind … ?

Match the questions with the answers.

1. What kind of things do you read?
2. What kind of things do you listen to?
3. What kind of things do you paint?
4. What kind of things do you go and see?
5. What kind of things do you collect?
6. What kind of things do you watch?

a. Anything really, but mainly Japanese pop music.
b. Anything really, but mainly old photographs and cameras. I've got about thirty different ones.
c. Anything really, but mainly programmes that make me laugh.
d. Anything really. Novels, biographies, history, poetry. You name it, I like it.
e. Mainly action movies. I love anything with Arnold Schwarzenegger in it.
f. Mainly portraits and sometimes I do pictures of animals.

5 Verbs

Complete the collocations with the verbs in the box. All the verbs are from the text *Family or friends* in the Coursebook.

argue	invite	ring	spend
chat	join	share	support

1. .... on the phone / to a friend / about what we did today
2. .... about politics / about money / about who's going to do the shopping
3. .... some friends to a party / a friend to my house for lunch / people to our wedding
4. .... a flat with two other people / a room / a pizza
5. .... all my money / a lot of time with my family / the night at a friend's house
6. .... Chelsea / my local team / my family when they need help
7. .... my friend for a chat / the cinema to book the tickets / work to tell them I'll be late
8. .... the army / a gym / a tennis club / us for a meal

6 How do you know each other?

Match each of the questions with two answers.

1. How do you know each other?
2. So how long have you known each other?
3. So what does she do?
4. Do you go out together much?

a. It must be almost 15 years now.
b. Yes, all the time. We probably see each other three or four times a week.
c. We went to the same school.
d. We lived in the same street when we were young.
e. She's a nurse.
f. Since we were kids.
g. Not as much as we used to. We both work very hard, so it's difficult to find time to meet up.
h. She runs her own company.

Language note: *run*

If you *run your own company*, you're the boss. You can also *run a family business, run a hotel, run a shop* and *run a restaurant*. We sometimes describe these places as *well-run* or *badly-run*.

7 Key word: go

Complete the conversations with the words in the box.

a friend	holiday	the toilet
ahead	own	to get
bed	round to	well
for	swimming	your exam

1. A: What are you doing tonight?

   B: I'm really tired. I'm just going to go to .... early. Why?

   A: Oh, I'm going .... later. I wanted you to come with me.

   B: Thanks, but I'm really tired. Maybe tomorrow.

   A: Yes, OK.

2. A: Are you going on .... in the summer?

   B: Yes, I'm going to Australia to study English.

   A: Really, that's great. Are you going on your .... ?

   B: No, I'm going with .... of mine.

   A: Lovely.

3. A: What did you do yesterday?

   B: I went .... a friend's house to have lunch. What about you?

   A: Oh, I went .... a walk round town.

   B: That sounds nice.

   A: Yes, it was.

4. A: I'm just going .... a newspaper. Do you want anything from the shop?

   B: No thanks. I'm fine.

5. A: Is it OK if I open the window?

   B: Yes, sure. Go ....

6. A: Where's John?

   B: He's just gone to .... He'll be back in a moment.

7. A: How did .... go?

   B: Oh, I think it went really .... I'm sure I passed.

   A: I hope so.

8 Too

Choose the correct word.

1. It's too *near / far* to drive. It's only round the corner.

2. It's too *near / far* to walk. It'll take too long.

3. It's too *hot / cold* to eat inside. Let's go outside.

4. It's too *hot / cold* to eat now. Wait a minute.

5. It's too *early / late* to go. I don't want to be the first one to arrive.

6. It's too *early / late* to go now. The film will've started.

7. I'm too *old / young* to start a new career now.

8. I'm too *old / young* to retire. I could work for another ten years.

9. This new job is a great opportunity for me. It's too *good / bad* to miss.

10. It was a mistake, but it's too *late / soon* to do anything about it now.

9 Too fast / too much

Complete the sentences with the pairs of words in the box.

a car crash + drives
a heart attack + works
a stomach-ache + ate
annoys + talks
can't understand + talks
get to sleep + were playing
makes + does
weight + eats

1. He's put on a lot of .... He .... too much.

2. I .... what she says. She .... too fast.

3. She .... a lot of mistakes because she .... things too quickly.

4. I couldn't .... last night because my neighbours .... their music too loud.

5. I've got .... I think I .... that sandwich too quickly.

6. He really .... a lot of people in the class. He .... too much.

7. He's going to have .... one day. He .... too fast.

8. He's going to have .... if he's not careful. He .... too hard.

10 Pen friends

Choose the correct words to complete this letter.

Dear Nelson,

I (1) .... your advert on the International Friends website looking for a pen friend and I (2) .... like to start writing to you. Let me tell you a bit (3) .... myself. My name is Zana. I am a 16-year-old student from Slovenia, which in case you didn't know is between Croatia and Italy. I am from the capital, Ljubljana. I live with my mum and my two sisters, (4) .... are both younger than me. I have two more years at school and then I'm (5) .... to go to university to study English. I'd like to teach English eventually or maybe become a translator. I like (6) .... – mainly novels – and I collect cuddly toys. I also like listening to music. I'm a big (7) .... of the Beatles.

Please write to me and tell me more about yourself. I'm sure we'll have a lot (8) .... !

Zana

1. A saw	B viewed	C looked	D watched
2. A would	B am	C do	D want
3. A to	B about	C for	D with
4. A that	B which	C who	D whom
5. A hoping	B wanting	C will	D want
6. A dancing	B watching TV	C films	D reading
7. A lover	B supporter	C fan	D like
8. A the same	B in common	C similar	D loves

Write a reply to Zana's letter.

11 Would you like ... ? / Do you like ... ?

Do you know the difference between the two questions above?

Would you like ... ? asks about the future. It means 'Do you want ... ?' We usually reply *Yes, please* or *No, thanks* and we often add an extra comment. *Do you like ... ?* asks about general preferences.

Complete the conversations with *Do you like* or *Would you like*.

1. A: I'm thinking of going for a swim later.
   .... to come?
   B: Thanks for asking, but I can't. I'm going out.

2. A: .... sport?
   B: No, I hate it! It's so boring. Why do men talk about it so much?

3. A: .... to go to the cinema with me later?
   B: Yes, OK. What's on?

4. A: .... going to the cinema?
   B: Yes, I love it. I usually go at least twice a week.

5. A: .... a coffee?
   B: No, thanks. I've just had one.

6. A: .... coffee?
   B: Not really. I usually drink tea.

7. A: .... Tony Joe White?
   B: Yes, he's OK, I suppose, but I don't have any of his CDs.

8. A: .... some cake?
   B: Yes, please. It looks delicious.

3 Have you got ... ?

1 Have you got a / any ... ?

Complete the sentences with the pairs of words in the box.

cloth + spilt	pen + write down
correction fluid + made	plasters + cut
dictionary + means	screwdriver + unscrew

1. Oh no! Have you got a .... ? I've just
   .... wine all over your carpet.

2. Ouch! Have you got any .... ? I've just
   .... myself.

3. Have you got a .... ? I need to
   .... this phone number before I forget.

4. Have you got a .... ? I just need to
   .... the back of this toy so I can
   change the batteries.

5. Have you got any .... ? I've just
   .... a mistake.

6. Have you got a .... ? I want to know
   what 'plumber' ....

Now match the responses with the sentences above.

1. ☐   2. ☐   3. ☐   4. ☐   5. ☐   6. ☐

a. Oh no! We haven't got any. I'll get you a cloth to put
   on it until it stops bleeding.

b. Don't worry. I'll do it. It's an old carpet anyway.

c. Sorry, I haven't got one. Tell me it and I'll help you to
   remember it.

d. No, I haven't, but you don't need to look it up. It's
   the person who fixes taps and toilets and things like
   that.

e. Sorry, I've lost it. I can get you a knife to do it,
   though.

f. Sorry, I haven't. Just cross it out. It doesn't matter.

2 One / some

Complete the conversations with *one* or *some*.

1. A: Have you got any milk?
   B: Yes, there's .... in the fridge.

2. A: Have you got any sugar?
   B: Yes, of course. I'll just get .... for you.

3. A: Have you got a spoon?
   B: Sorry, didn't I give you .... ? I'll just go
      and get ....

4. A: Have you got a rubber?
   B: Yes, there's .... in my pencil case
      there. Just take it.

5. A: Have you got any paper?
   B: Yes, there's .... on the desk in the study.

6. A: Have you got an English-English dictionary?
   B: Yes, there's .... on the shelf at the
      back of the class.

3 Things in the house

Look at the pictures. Find the things in the house.

shelves	☐	kitchen table	☐	fridge	☐
wardrobe	☐	top drawer	☐	desk	☐
cupboard	☐	bottom drawer	☐	sink	☐

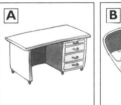
A

B

C

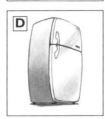
D

E

F

G

H
I

4 Prepositions of place

Complete the sentences with *in*, *on* or *under*.

1. It's .... one of the drawers .... the kitchen.

2. It's .... the cupboard .... the stairs.

3. It's .... the top shelf .... the kitchen.

4. It's .... the table .... the front room.

5. It's .... a box .... the garage.

6. It's .... my bag.

7. They're .... a pile .... the corner of my bedroom.

8. They're .... the floor .... the hall.

5 Conversation

Complete the conversation with ONE word in each space.

P: Ouch!

S: What's up?

P: I've (1) .... cut my finger on this nail.

S: Let's (2) .... a look. Oh, yes. That's quite nasty.

P: I'd (3) .... run it under the tap.

S: Have you got any plasters? I'll go and get you one.

P: Yes, I think there are some (4) .... the shelf in the bathroom.

S: I can't see (5) .... Are you sure they're here?

P: Do you see the cupboard by the bath? Have a look in there. I think there are some in the top drawer.

S: I've (6) .... them.

P: Thanks.

S: I also found these.

P: Oh, er … right … er … Where did you find those?

S: They (7) .... on the floor.

P: Whose are they?

S: Well, they're not (8) .... !

Language note: *break* and *tear*

You can *break* glasses, *plates*, *windows* and *bones* in your body. You can also *break* cameras, mobile phones and *watches* if you drop them. You can *tear your clothes* and you can also *tear a muscle*. The adjectives are *broken* and *torn*.

6 Oh no!

Complete the sentences with the words in the box.

cut	forgotten	lost	torn
dropped	left	spilt	

1. Oh no! I've .... wine all over the carpet!

2. Oh no! I've .... my PIN number!

3. Oh no! I've .... my travel card at home!

4. Oh no! I've .... my address book! There were lots of important numbers in it.

5. Ouch! I've just .... myself!

6. Oh no! I've .... my shirt on a nail!

7. Oh no! I've just .... a glass on the floor! Be careful!

7 Everyday things

Complete the questions with the names of the things in the pictures.

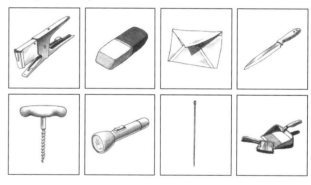

1. Have you got a .... and .... ? I've spilt some sugar on the floor and want to clean it up.

2. Have you got a .... ? I just want to keep all these papers together.

3. Have you got an .... ? I need one so I can send this letter off.

4. Have you got a .... ? I want to open this bottle of wine.

5. Have you got a .... ? A button has come off my shirt and I want to put it back on.

6. Have you got a .... ? I've made a mistake with this letter. I need to write this bit again.

7. Have you got a .... ? I want to go outside into the garden, but it's really dark out there.

8. Have you got a .... ? I want to chop these vegetables.

8 I'm thinking of ...

Match the invitations with the replies.

1. I'm thinking of going to see an opera while I'm here. Would you like to come? ☐

2. I'm thinking of going to see a play while I'm in London. Would you like to come? ☐

3. I'm thinking of going to see the King Kurt concert when they play here. Would you like to come? ☐

4. I'm thinking of going to see the Dali exhibition while I'm here. Would you like to come? ☐

5. I'm thinking of going to see Manchester United play while I'm here. Would you like to come? ☐

6. I'm thinking of going to the mountains while I'm here. Would you like to come? ☐

a. No, thanks. I don't really like their music.
b. No, thanks. I don't really like going to art galleries.
c. No, thanks. I don't really like walking.
d. No, thanks. I don't really like football.
e. No, thanks. I don't really like classical music.
f. No, thanks. I don't really like going to the theatre.

9 Explaining decisions

Complete the sentences with the words in the box.

breaking down	falling	repair
burn	get on with	use
contact	park	

1. I need to get a new computer. I can't .... the latest software on the one I've got now.

2. I'm thinking of getting a new computer. I can't .... my own DVDs on the one I've got now.

3. I need to get a new bike. The one I've got now is .... to pieces.

4. I need to get a new TV. The one I've got now isn't working and it'll cost too much to .... it.

5. I'm thinking of getting a new car. The one I've got now keeps ....

6. I'm thinking of getting a smaller car. It'll be easier to .... in town and it'll use less petrol.

7. I'm thinking of getting a new job. I don't .... my boss. He's so rude.

8. I'm thinking of getting a mobile for my wife. I'd like to be able to .... her during the day.

10 Questions and answers

Match the questions with the answers.

1. Have you got a car? ☐
2. Have you got any children? ☐
3. Have you got a computer at home? ☐
4. Have you got a mobile phone? ☐
5. Have you got any brothers or sisters? ☐
6. Have you got any pets? ☐
7. Have you got a degree? ☐

a. Yes, I have. One of each. One older than me, one younger.
b. No, but we've got one in the office, so I can use the e-mail there.
c. Yes, I have. I graduated last year in French and Italian.
d. Yes, I have. I've got a hamster called Noel.
e. No, but I have got a scooter. I use that to get into work every day.
f. No, I haven't. My wife and I can't have any, actually.
g. No, not any more. I left my last one on the bus.

11 Which one? That one!

We often use *one / ones* to refer to something when it has already been mentioned in the conversation, or when we think the person we are talking to will know what we mean.

Choose the correct form.

1. I don't really like that shirt. I prefer *the one / the ones* you tried on earlier. It was brighter.
2. I don't really like those boots. I prefer *the one / the ones* you tried on in that other shop.
3. I didn't like his second book. *The first one / The first ones* was much better.
4. I've got to buy some new headphones for this Walkman. *This one / These ones* don't work properly any more.
5. I really need to get some new clothes. *The one / The ones* I've brought with me aren't warm enough.
6. I really need to get some new jeans. *This one / These ones* are falling to pieces.
7. I don't really like their new flat. *The one / The ones* they had before was much better.
8. I don't really like this car. I perfer *the one / the ones* you've got. It's much easier to drive.

12 Key words for writing: *but* and *though*

We connect different or opposite ideas with *but* or *though*. We use different grammar with each word. For example:

- I'm really busy this week, *but* I haven't got much planned for next week, so let's meet then.
- I'm really busy this week. I haven't got much planned for next week, *though*, so let's meet then.

Complete the sentences with *but* or *though*.

1. I would really love to study more English, ... I don't have enough free time.

2. I'd love to come and visit you this weekend, ... it's my dad's 60th birthday and he's having a big party.

3. I'd love to come to your wedding, but I have to work that day. I can come to the party in the evening, ... I'm really excited about it!

4. Just a quick e-mail to say I can't come to the meeting tomorrow because I'm going on holiday. I'll be back Thursday next week, ... , so maybe we could have a meeting then.

5. I had my mobile phone stolen yesterday, so you can't ring me on that number any more! You can phone me on my work mobile, ... The number is 0897 63542.

6. I'm not coming to work today, because I've got a bit of an upset stomach, ... hopefully, I'll be back tomorrow.

But and though are also very common in spoken English. For example:

A: Did you go to the class yesterday?
B: Yes. You didn't miss anything, *though*. It was really boring.
A: Did you go to the class yesterday?
B: Yes, *but* you didn't miss anything. It was really boring.

13 Writing e-mails

Complete the e-mails with the words in the box.

best	congratulations	love	thank you
but	e-mail	send	though

Hi Billy and Jean,

Just a quick e-mail to say (1) .... for letting me stay last weekend. It was great to see you and I had a really nice time. I've just come back from the photo shop and I've got some nice pictures, which I'm going to (2) .... to you in the post.

Lots of (3) .... , Martina

Dear Mark and Diane,

Just a quick e-mail to say (4) .... on your new baby girl. I'm sorry I haven't written earlier (5) .... I've been really busy travelling. I'm at home this week (6) .... , so I'd like to come and see you all, if that's OK. (7) .... me to let me know a convenient time for you.

All the (8) .... , Elton

14 Starting letters and e-mails

Complete the sentence endings with the words in the box.

doing	moved	studying
looking for	sorry	thanks

Sorry I haven't written to you recently, but I've been busy ...

1. .... a new job.

2. .... for my exams.

3. .... lots of things for work.

Just a quick e-mail to ...

4. tell you I've .... house and to give you my new address.

5. say .... for the lovely dinner you cooked last night.

6. say .... , but I can't come to the party.

Now write your own e-mail using one of the starter phrases.

4 Times and dates

1 Do you know what the time is?

Complete the times.

1. It's a quarter ....
2. It's half ....
3. It's ten ....
4. It's twenty ....
5. It's just gone ....
6. It's almost ....
7. It's almost ....
8. It's just gone ....
9. It's almost ....

①	②	③

④	⑤	⑥

⑦	⑧	⑨

Language note

Sometimes we say *my watch is slow*. (It says it's ten o'clock, but it's really ten past ten.) The opposite is *my watch is fast*.

2 Conversation

Complete the conversation with ONE word in each space.

S: Are you (1) .... to the party for new students tonight?

E: I think so. And you?

S: Yes, it (2) .... be nice to meet a few new people.

E: Yes, and it's free!

S: Exactly. I never say (3) .... to anything that's free.

E: What time (4) .... it start?

S: Seven, but I'm going a bit (5) .... I don't want to be the first one there.

E: Neither do I. I hate going to places on my (6) ....

S: Do you (7) .... to meet up before, and then we could go together?

E: Yes, great. Where (8) .... we meet?

S: How about the café next to the school? We (9) .... have a drink first.

E: Yes, OK. What time?

S: How (10) .... a quarter past seven? We don't want to miss all the food and drink.

E: OK. That (11) .... fine.

S: What're you doing now? Have you got (12) .... for a coffee?

E: I don't know. What time is it?

S: Just (13) .... half past nine.

E: Half past nine? Oh, I've got to go. I'm late for my class.

S: OK. Well, I'll see you in the café at quarter past seven, then.

E: OK. Bye.

Can you remember where the pauses and the stressed sounds were in this conversation? Mark the pauses // and underline the stressed syllables. For example:

A: Are you going to the <u>par</u>ty // for new <u>stu</u>dents // to<u>night</u>?

B: I <u>think</u> so. // And <u>you</u>?

Compare your ideas about the pauses and stressed sounds with the tapescript in the Coursebook.

3 What are you doing at the weekend? – present continuous or *might*

When we've arranged to do something with someone else, we normally use the verb in the present continuous. When we do not know exactly or when we are not sure, we normally use *might*.

Complete the sentences with the present continuous form of the verb or *might* + verb.

1. I .... (meet) a friend for dinner on Saturday night. We're going to an Italian place.

2. I'm not sure. I .... (go) for a picnic with my family on Sunday. It depends on the weather.

3. Some friends .... (come) over to my house for dinner tomorrow, so I need to do some shopping.

4. I don't really know. A friend of mine said he .... (come) over to play chess tomorrow, but he's not sure.

5. I don't know. I think I .... (go) to the cinema tomorrow. I'd like to see Gun Boys.

6. I .... (go) to the Shaft concert tonight with a friend. She bought me a ticket for my birthday.

7. We .... (have) a party for my birthday. Do you want to come?

8. I .... (go) to my brother's wedding on Saturday, but I haven't got any plans for Sunday.

9. A friend from Turkey .... (come) to stay. She .... (arrive) this afternoon, actually.

10. I'm not sure. I think we .... (have) a barbecue on Sunday, though. I'll phone you if we do.

Spend five minutes memorising the collocations which are underlined. Can you find any more verb + noun collocations in the sentences?

4 Making arrangements

Put the sentences in order and make conversations.

Conversation 1

a. I'm going shopping. Do you want to come?

b. Yes, OK. What time?

c. What are you doing later?

d. That sounds fine. I'll see you there then.

e. My class finishes at one, so how about quarter past one, just outside the main entrance?

1. ☐   2. ☐   3. ☐   4. ☐   5. ☐

Conversation 2

a. Well, it starts at eight, so how about around seven at Tom's Diner? We could go and have a coffee first.

b. What are you doing tonight?

c. Yes, that sounds fine. I'll see you there then.

d. Yes, OK. What time?

e. I'm going to the cinema to see *The Beast*. Do you want to come?

1. ☐   2. ☐   3. ☐   4. ☐   5. ☐

Conversation 3

a. I'm sorry, I can't. Some friends are coming round for lunch.

b. Yes. Are you doing anything next weekend?

c. We're going on a trip to Oxford on Sunday. Do you want to come?

d. What are you doing at the weekend?

e. Oh well, never mind. Some other time, maybe.

1. ☐   2. ☐   3. ☐   4. ☐   5. ☐

Test yourself. Spend five minutes memorising the conversations. Then close your book and write as much as you can remember on a piece of paper. How much did you get right?

5 | Verbs that go with *time*

Complete the sentences with the words in the box.

arrange	have	have	's	spent	takes

1. It .... a long time to learn a language well. You need to be patient.

2. Do you .... time to talk now? I have a few questions I want to ask you.

3. A: We must meet up some time.
   B: Yes. Shall we .... a time and date now? I've got my diary here.

4. A: I'm going on holiday to Greece tomorrow.
   B: Lucky you! Well, I hope you .... a nice time.

5. A: Did you have a nice holiday?
   B: Yes, it was great. We .... most of our time on the beach. It was really relaxing.

6. A: Don't go home yet. It's only three o'clock!
   B: No. I'm going. It .... well past my bedtime. I'm usually in bed by eleven!

6 | I'll always remember it

Choose the correct words to complete this text.

I'll never (1) .... the day my daughter Rebecca was born. My wife didn't go to hospital to (2) .... the baby. She gave birth at home, so it was very (3) .... – just me, my wife and a female doctor. My wife started to (4) .... pains at around eight o'clock in the evening and Rebecca was born (5) .... four o'clock in the morning, so the birth (6) .... about eight hours. My wife made a lot of (7) .... She was really screaming when the baby was coming out and at one (8) .... our neighbour came round to (9) .... she was OK! When I saw Rebecca, it was just amazing. I'll always remember it. It's the most amazing (10) .... I've had in my life.

1. A remember	B forget	C remind	D realise
2. A have	B born	C pregnant	D birth
3. A close	B private	C particular	D happy
4. A give	B be	C feel	D make
5. A at	B in	C of	D on
6. A took	B last	C continued	D was
7. A mess	B loud	C shouting	D noise
8. A period	B time	C moments	D point
9. A find	B look	C check	D know
10. A experiment	B memory	D experience	D moment

7 | Special days

Complete the sentences with the words in the box.

Independence Day	Valentine's Day
my birthday	wedding anniversary
public holiday	

1. I'm having a party on Friday to celebrate
   .... I'll be 21.

2. It's .... on November 11th. We used to be a colony of Britain, but we became independent 35 years ago.

3. It's .... next week. I'm going to send my girlfriend twelve red roses!

4. My parents have been married for almost 50 years. It's their golden .... next year.

5. We should go to the supermarket today. It's a .... tomorrow, so everywhere will be closed.

8 | I hope

Complete the sentences with the correct form of the verbs in the box. (The last three sentences need negative verbs!)

be	get	lose	rain
be	like	pass	win

1. Good luck with the exam. I hope you ....

2. Good luck with the job interview. I hope you .... the job.

3. I hate Real Madrid. I hope they .... on Saturday.

4. I love Real Madrid. I hope they .... on Saturday.

5. I'm meeting my girlfriend's father for the first time. I hope he .... me.

6. I'm driving to Birmingham. I hope the traffic .... too bad.

7. We're going for a picnic. I hope it ....

8. I'm meeting a friend at the airport later. I hope his flight .... delayed.

9 Time expressions

Complete the sentences with the words in the box.

in	other	tomorrow
minute	sometime	week

1. Can you wait for me? I'll be ready in a
   .... or two.

2. Hopefully, I'm going to go to China ....
   next year, but I don't know when exactly.

3. Did I tell you? I saw Marianne the ....
   day. She asked me to say hello.

4. I'm going to go back home to my country the day
   after ....

5. You know I applied for a new job. Well, I got it! So I'll
   be starting .... a few weeks' time.

6. It's my birthday a .... today.

10 What are they going to do?

Match the sentences with the speakers.

1. Just take a bit off, please, and tidy it up. ☐
2. They've got a sale on at the moment. ☐
3. I'm sure he's going to tell me I have to have
   some fillings or a tooth taken out. ☐
4. I really need some time on my own, so I can
   just lie around and do nothing. ☐
5. I'm really nervous. This is the fifth time
   I've had to retake it. ☐

a. He's going to go on holiday.
b. He's having his hair cut.
c. He's going to retake his driving test.
d. She's going to go to the dentist.
e. She's going to go shopping.

Language note: *go on holiday*

Usually, when people *go on holiday*, they go to a
different city or country for a week or two weeks. If
you don't have much time, you can just *go away for the
weekend*. Maybe you *go to Paris for the weekend* or *go to
the countryside for the weekend*. If you don't have much
time, you can just *go on a day trip*.

11 Key word: *look*

**Complete the sentences with *a look, look* or
looking.**

1. If you don't know what any of the words mean,
   .... them up in your dictionary or ask me.

2. A: Are you .... forward to the
      holidays?
   B: Yes. I can't wait. We're going to China. It should
      be great.

3. A: What are you going to do with your dog while
      you're on holiday?
   B: My neighbour is going to .... after it.
      He's going to feed it and take it out every day.

4. A: Can I have .... at your newspaper
      a moment? I want to see what's on TV tonight.
   B: Yes, of course. Go ahead.

5. A: Have you found a new place to live?
   B: No. I've been to .... at five or six flats,
      but they were either too small or too expensive.

6. A: Excuse me, I'm .... for a bookshop
      called Waterstones. Do you know where it is?
   B: Yes, it's just off this road. Keep going until you
      come to the traffic lights. It's on your left.

7. A: What are you going to do this afternoon?
   B: We're going to have .... round the
      old part of town. We've heard there are lots of
      things to see there.

8. A: Do you want to go to the Italian restaurant?
   B: No. I've never been in there, but it doesn't
      .... very nice.

**Translate the underlined expressions into your
language.**

1. Look a word up in your dictionary.

   ....

2. I'm looking forward to my holiday.

   ....

3. Have a look at the newspaper.

   ....

4. Have a look round a museum.

   ....

5. I'm looking for a place called Café Nero.

   ....

6. It doesn't look very nice.

   ....

7. A friend is looking after the children tonight.

   ....

5 Buying things

1 Clothes

Complete the conversations with the words in the box.

boots	suit and tie	trainers
bracelet	sunglasses	T-shirt
coat	swimsuit	

1. A: I'd like to go running, but I didn't pack my
   ....

   B: What size shoes do you take? I might be able
   to lend you some.

2. A: I didn't realise there was a pool at the hotel.
   I didn't pack my ....

   B: That's a shame. It looks really nice. Maybe you
   could buy a cheap one.

3. A: I like your .... Is it real gold?

   B: Yes. I got it when I was 14. It's actually a bit tight
   round my wrist now, but I still like it.

4. A: Aren't you cold just wearing
   a .... ?

   B: Not at all. It's hot!

5. A: I wasn't expecting it to be sunny here at
   this time of year.

   B: I know. I didn't pack my ....
   The sun's really getting in my eyes.

6. A: Do you think I'll need to wear ....
   when we go for this walk?

   B: I'm going to. It can be quite muddy.

7. A: Do you think I'll need a .... ?

   B: No. It's quite mild.

8. A: Do I need to wear a .... ?

   B: No, it's going to be quite an informal party.

Language note: *mild*

Mild has several different meanings. If you have a *mild winter* or *it's mild for the time of year*, it's not very cold. *Mild cheese* is not very strong and a *mild curry* is not very spicy. If you just have a *mild infection* or a *mild cold*, it's not very bad and you probably don't need any drugs to treat it.

2 Describing people

Here are four ways to identify a person without pointing at them.

1. using an adjective:
   You see <u>that fat guy</u>.

2. adding *with* + a physical feature or clothes:
   You see <u>that guy *with the beard and glasses*</u>.

3. adding a prepositional phrase explaining where
   the person is:
   You see the <u>woman *next to Peter*</u>.

4. adding a verb in the -ing form to explain what
   the person is doing:
   You see the <u>woman *combing her hair*</u>.

Note we use *that* or *the* to describe the person and the feature because we are talking about one specific person and thing.

Complete the sentences using the ideas in brackets and the structures above. The first one has been done for you.

1. (woman / she's tall / she's got a blue dress)
   Hey, you see <u>*the tall woman with the blue dress*</u> .
   Do you think she's wearing a wig?

2. (guy / he's short / he's got dark hair)
   Hey, you see ....
   and the leather jacket. Isn't that Tom Cruise?

3. (guy / he's got dark glasses / he's got a long coat)
   Hey, you see ....
   standing by the doors. Do you think he's a spy?

4. (woman / she's thin / she's got blond hair)
   Hey, you see .... at
   the table next to us. Isn't that Madonna?

5. (guy / he's fat / he's got tight jeans / he's standing
   over there)
   Hey, you see ....
   Do you think he's got a gun in his pocket?

6. (woman / she's got long brown hair / she's at the
   table by the window)
   Hey, you see ....
   Isn't that Katy's sister?

7. (man / he's tall / he's got glasses / he's talking to the
   black woman)
   Hey, you see ....
   Isn't that Tom Hanks?

3 | Conversation

Translate these expressions into your language.

a. Whereabouts exactly ....

b. thanks for telling me ....

c. I can imagine ....

d. Are they new? ....

e. it's about halfway down ....

f. They've got a sale on ....

g. reduced from 65 ....

h. to begin with ....

i. I just couldn't resist them. ....

j. They really suit you. ....

Now complete the conversation with the expressions.

C: Oh, I like those shoes. (1) ....

L: Yes, I only bought them a few days ago.

C: They're really nice. (2) ....

L: Thanks. I wasn't sure about them
(3) .... , but I really like them now.

C: Yes, I love the design. Where did you get them?

L: From this great shop in Hockley. (4) ....
at the moment, and (5) ....

C: (6) .... How much were they?

L: They were 29.99, (7) ....

C: Wow! That's brilliant! (8) .... is
this shop? I might try to go there later.

L: Well, do you know where Castle Street is?

C: Yes, I think so.

L: Well, as you're going down the hill, (9) .... ,
on the left. I think it's called Barrett's.

C: Oh right. Well, (10) ....

L: That's OK. Let me know if you buy anything!

Can you remember where the pauses and the stressed sounds are in this conversation? Mark the pauses // and <u>underline</u> the stressed syllables. For example:

A: Oh, I like those shoes. // Are they new?
B: Yes, // I only bought them // a few days ago.

Compare your ideas about the pauses and stressed sounds with the tapescript in the Coursebook.

4 | I got it in the sale

Complete the sentences with the words in the box.

get one free	reduced from	staff discount
half-price	sell-by-date	ten per cent
off	special offer	

1. It was .... They're usually
£50, but I got it for £25.

2. It was £50 – .... £80.

3. You buy one and you ....

4. They were on .... It had
£10 .... They're
usually £15, but I got it for five.

5. I get a .... because I work
there.

6. If you show them your student card, you get a
.... discount.

7. All the food was reduced because it was almost past
its ....

5 | I need to do some housework

Complete the sentences with the words in the box.

hoovering	repairs	tidying up
ironing	shopping	washing

1. I haven't got any clean clothes. I need to do some
....

2. There's no food in the fridge. I need to do some
....

3. My shirts are all creased. I need to do some
....

4. There are crumbs all over the carpet. I need to do
some ....

5. My room's in a mess and there are papers all over
the house. I need to do some ....

6. The house is falling apart. I need to do some
....

6 Enough

Rewrite the sentences with *enough*. The first one has been done for you.

1. The interview was awful! They told me I didn't have qualifications.
   They told me I didn't have enough qualifications.

2. I left my last job because the money wasn't good.

3. I'd like to get a ticket for the concert, but I don't have money.

4. This doesn't taste right. It's not sweet.

5. I didn't finish my homework. I didn't have time.

6. The public transport here is terrible! There aren't buses or trains!

7. I'm afraid I can't play tennis today. I don't feel well.

8. I don't really like this kind of music. It's not fast.

7 I can't! It's too big.

Match the problems with the reasons.

1. I can't afford this bracelet.
2. I can't drink this coffee.
3. I can't wear this top.
4. I can't do this exercise.
5. I can't eat this beef!
6. I can't hear the tape.
7. I can't go to school today.
8. I can't vote in the election.

a. It's too tight.
b. It's too difficult.
c. It's too quiet.
d. I'm too young.
e. I'm too ill.
f. It's too spicy.
g. It's too expensive.
h. It's too strong.

Language note: *vote*

You can *vote in a general election* in Britain when you are 18. You *vote for your local MP* (member of parliament), but you can't vote for the Prime Minster. The Prime Minister is the leader of the party which *gets the most votes*. You *vote for a political party*. You can also *vote in favour of* an idea or *against* an idea.

8 Not enough

Complete the sentences with the words in the box.

big	clever	good	rich
brave	fit	long	tall

1. Can you reach that book for me? The one on the top shelf. I'm not .... enough to get it!

2. A: This shirt doesn't fit me. It's not .... enough.
   B: I can see that. It looks really tight.

3. I'd like to go and work in Australia for a year, but my English isn't .... enough.

4. I'd love to apply to Oxford or Cambridge University, but I'm not .... enough to get in.

5. I wanted to ask her if she had a boyfriend, but I wasn't .... enough. I'm so shy!

6. I'd love to take a year off and travel the world, but I'm not .... enough. I can't even afford a holiday!

7. I'd like to cycle to work, but I'm not .... enough. I haven't done any exercise for years!

8. A: How long did you stay in Morocco?
   B: Not .... enough! It was only six days.

9 Asking negative questions

Match the negative questions with the responses.

1. Don't you think this book is a bit too expensive?
2. Don't you think it's cold in here?
3. Don't you think she looks ridiculous in that dress?
4. Don't you think his hair looks terrible?
5. Don't you think the boss looks really scruffy?
6. Don't you think Lee is a bit boring?

a. Yes, maybe a bit. Do you want me to turn the heating on?
b. Yes, maybe a bit, but I don't look very smart either!
c. Yes, maybe it was better before he had it cut and dyed.
d. No, not at all. I think she looks quite trendy. It suits her.
e. No, not at all. I think it's good value for money.
f. No, not really. I find him quite interesting usually.

10 Key words for writing: also, too and as well

All of these words mean the same thing, but the grammar is different. *Too / as well* are more common in spoken English. For example:

- He's got a degree in Physics and he *also* speaks three languages.
- He's got a degree in Physics and he speaks three languages *too*.
- He's got a degree in Physics and he speaks three languages *as well*.

Rewrite the sentences with the adverb in brackets.

1. I study very hard, but I like playing golf. (too)

   ....

2. I like reading and writing, and I do photography. (also)

   ....

3. I go out a lot, but I like staying in and reading. (as well)

   ....

4. I have a degree in computer science and I have a Master's in business management. (also)

   ....

5. There are lots of cafés and pubs near where I live and there's a big cinema. (as well)

   ....

6. The university has a large library and a sports centre, and it has a modern conference centre. (also)

   ....

Language note: as well

As *well as* is sometimes used to join two ideas instead of *and* or *but*. For example:
As well as having a degree in Physics, he speaks three languages.
As well as studying very hard, I like playing golf.

Rewrite the sentences above using *as well as*.

2. ....

3. ....

4. ....

5. ....

6. ....

11 Writing – personal statements

When you apply to do a university course, you often have to write a personal statement saying why you want to do the course, why you would be good at the course, why you want to do the course at that particular place and what you plan to do afterwards. You also usually give some idea of the kind of person you are and your general likes and interests.

Complete the personal statements with the words in the box.

especially	specialist courses
first prize	taught myself
free time	too
interested	want

I really (1) .... to do the course in computer science because I have always been very (2) .... in computing. As well as studying information technology at school, I have (3) .... several programming languages such as Javascript, C+ and Pascal. I also make robots in my (4) .... Last year I won (5) .... in the final of the competition *Robot Wars*. I have also done well at school. I got five top grades in my final exams.

I am quite friendly and like meeting new people. I am a member of a local video game club and I like going to concerts (6) .... I really like heavy metal and grunge music.

I would (7) .... like to study at North Midland University, because it has a very good reputation for computer science and because you have (8) .... in robotics, which I am really interested in. After the course, I would like to work for a big electronics company.

Now write a personal statement for a course you would like to do. Try to use some of these sentence starters:

- I really want to do the course in …
- I have always been very interested in …
- As well as … , I …
- I have also done well at school. I got …
- I would especially like to study at … because …
- After the course, I would like to …

6 How are you?

1 I'm a bit fed up

If you're *fed up*, you are angry and bored because something bad has been going on for too long. For example:

A: How are you?

B: To be honest, I'm a bit fed up.

A: Oh, no! Why?

B: It's my English! I don't feel it's getting any better. I keep making the same mistakes!

Complete the sentences with the expressions in the box. Use each expression twice.

my English	the flat we're renting
my job	the weather
my mum and dad	these classes

1. It's .... I don't feel it's getting any better. I keep making the same mistakes!

2. It's .... I'm really missing them. I haven't seen them for six months.

3. It's .... It's so cold and wet.

4. It's .... I'm bored with doing the same things every day for so little money.

5. It's .... It's so hot, I can't sleep at night.

6. It's .... We're having a lot of problems with the landlord.

7. It's .... I don't really like the teacher.

8. It's .... I can never find the words to say what I want. It's really frustrating.

9. It's .... They're always telling me what to do!

10. It's .... I don't really like the people I work with.

11. It's .... The central heating's broken down – and it's really cold.

12. It's .... It's just so boring doing the same kind of exercises every day.

Test yourself. Spend five minutes memorising the sentences. Then close your book and write as much as you can remember on a piece of paper. How much did you get right?

Language note: *break down*

It's horrible if the central heating *breaks down* in the winter. *Cars break down, buses break down, photocopiers break down, lifts break down.* When things *break down*, you *need to get them fixed* by paying a mechanic or a technician, or by asking a friend who is good at fixing things.

2 Conversation (1)

Put the sentences in order and make a conversation.

a. Oh no! What's the problem?

b. I'm fine. What about you? You weren't in class today. I'm just phoning to make sure you're OK.

c. Oh no! I'm sorry. Have you been to see anyone about it?

d. Yes, hi. How are you?

e. Oh, thanks. That's really nice of you. I'm not very well, actually.

f. Hello. Is that Sarah?

g. No, I'll be all right. I just need to stay in bed for a while. I already feel a bit better than I did this morning.

h. I've got a really bad cold. I've been in bed all day.

1. ☐   2. ☐   3. ☐   4. ☐

5. ☐   6. ☐   7. ☐   8. ☐

Complete each expression from the conversation with ONE word.

i. make .... you're OK

j. That's really .... of you.

k. I'm not .... well

l. I feel a .... better

m. been in bed .... day

28

3 Questions and answers

Complete the conversations with the pairs of words in the box.

bad + days	painkillers + better
bug + sick	weak + easy
hospital + fine	

1. A: What's the problem?
   B: I've just got this horrible stomach
   .... I've been .... all night.

2. A: What's the problem?
   B: I've got this really .... cough. I've
   had it for ....

3. A: I've got a bit of a headache.
   B: Oh really? Have you taken anything for it?
   A: Yes, I took some .... earlier, and
   I'm feeling a bit .... now.

4. A: My back feels very strange.
   B: Really? Have you been to see anyone about it?
   A: Yes, I went to the .... this morning,
   but they said it was ....

5. A: I just feel really .... and tired. I've
   been in bed all day.
   B: Have you been to see anyone about it?
   A: Yes, I went to the doctor yesterday afternoon
   and he just told me to take it ....

4 Infinitives of purpose

Match the sentence beginnings with the endings.

1. I'm just phoning to ask ☐
2. I'm just phoning to make sure ☐
3. I'm just phoning to apologise ☐
4. I'm just phoning to let you know ☐
5. I'm just going out to the shops to buy ☐
6. I'm just going to the station to meet ☐
7. I've got to go to the dentist's to have ☐
8. I've got to go to work for an hour or two to finish off ☐

a. for what I said last night. I'm really sorry.
b. what you're doing this weekend.
c. a tooth out.
d. a report I'm writing for my boss.
e. my brother.
f. some milk and some coffee.
g. you got home OK last night.
h. I won't be able to come to the dinner tonight. Sorry.

5 Conversation (2)

Complete the conversation with the words in the box.

| actually | do | see | take |
| awful | kind | sounds | upset |

J: Hello.

T: Hi, Janet. It's Teresa. How's it going?

J: Great, thanks. How are you?

T: Not very well, (1) .... That's why I'm phoning. Can you tell Ralph I can't come to class tonight?

J: Yes, of course. What's the problem?

T: Oh, I've just got a really (2) .... stomach. I've been in and out of the bathroom all day.

J: Oh no, that's (3) .... ! I'm sorry. Can I (4) .... anything to help?

T: That's really (5) .... of you, but I'm all right. I'll be fine tomorrow.

J: Have you taken anything for it?

T: No, I'm just drinking lots of water and trying to (6) .... it easy.

J: Right, that (7) .... sensible.

T: Listen, I've got to go.

J: Yes, of course. I'll phone you tomorrow and (8) .... how you are.

T: OK. Thanks. Bye.

Can you remember where the pauses and the stressed sounds are in this conversation? Mark the pauses // and underline the stressed syllables. For example:

A: He<u>llo</u>.
B: Hi, <u>J</u>anet. // It's Te<u>re</u>sa. // How's it <u>go</u>ing?

Compare your ideas about the pauses and stressed sounds with the tapescript in the Coursebook.

6 I had a really late night

Match the sentence beginnings with the endings.

1. I'm really tired. I was up till three watching ☐
2. I'm really tired. I was up till half two chatting ☐
3. I'm really tired. I was up till two playing ☐
4. I'm really tired. I was up till four cleaning up ☐
5. I'm really tired. I was up till 1.30 finishing off ☐
6. I'm really tired. I was up till three sending ☐

a. to my sister on the phone.
b. a film on TV.
c. my flat. My girlfriend is coming to stay tomorrow.
d. e-mails to all my friends back home in my country.
e. an essay for my politics class.
f. computer games with a friend of mine.

Now match these sentence beginnings with the endings.

7. I'm really tired. I just couldn't get ☐
8. I'm really tired. I had to get up at five this morning ☐
9. I'm really tired. I went to the gym last night and did ☐
10. I'm really tired. I went out last night and got ☐
11. I'm really tired. I've worked ☐
12. I'm really tired. I've had ☐

g. to collect my daughter from the airport.
h. home at 3.30!
i. late every day this week!
j. a really busy day. I didn't even stop for lunch!
k. to sleep last night for some reason.
l. a bit too much.

Language note: *finish off*

If you *finish off an essay*, you finish it completely. You can also *finish off a report for your boss* and *finish off some things for work*. Near the end of a meal, you can also *finish off the rest of the food*.

7 Talking about sleeping

Complete the sentences with the words in the box.

asleep	overslept	wake up
fell asleep	stay awake	went to bed
had nightmares		

1. He was so tired, he .... while he was driving and crashed into a wall.
2. After I saw *Ghost Story 2*, I .... for weeks. It was such a scary film!
3. Sorry, but I didn't do my homework last night. I .... at 6.30. I wasn't feeling well.
4. I've got so much work to do this week! I had ten cups of coffee last night to help me .... and finish off an essay!
5. Sorry I'm late. I was so tired this morning, I .... I didn't .... until ten o'clock!
6. I lost my job because my boss found me .... at my desk – at two in the afternoon!

8 Can't / couldn't

Match the statements with the reasons.

1. I can't eat nuts. ☐
2. I can't drink alcohol. ☐
3. I can't drive. ☐
4. I can't play tennis with you next Tuesday. ☐
5. I couldn't ride a bike when I was younger. ☐
6. I couldn't really speak English last year. ☐
7. Women couldn't vote here until forty years ago. ☐
8. I couldn't go out with the other people from my class last Thursday. ☐

a. It used to be against the law. It's crazy, isn't it?
b. I wanted to, but I had to work late.
c. I failed my test twice – and then gave up!
d. I'm allergic to them. They make me really ill.
e. Now I can have quite a few basic conversations, though.
f. I'd like to, but I've got to work late.
g. It makes me feel really bad – and it makes my face go red too!
h. My mum taught me when I was eleven or twelve, though.

9 | What about you?

Complete the conversations with the responses in the box.

> I didn't, actually. I got woken up three or four times by the noise outside.
>
> I went to Berlin with my wife, actually. We only got back home at twelve last night.
>
> I'm meeting a friend, actually. I haven't seen her for ages.
>
> Oh, I haven't really been doing much, actually. Things have been quite quiet.
>
> Oh, I'm OK, thanks.

1. A: Did you sleep well?
   B: Yes, very. What about you?
   A: ....
   ....

2. A: Hi. Sorry I'm late. The traffic was terrible. Have you been waiting long?
   B: No, I've only just got here myself.
   A: So how's it going?
   B: Fine, what about you?
   A: ....
   ....

3. A: So what're you doing here? Are you doing some shopping or something?
   B: Yes, I am. What about you?
   A: ....
   ....

4. A: Did you have a good weekend?
   B: Yes, it was all right. I just stayed in and took it easy. What about you?
   A: ....
   ....

5. A: So what've you been doing recently?
   B: I've just been really busy with exams and studying. What about you?
   A: ....
   ....

Complete each expression from the conversations with ONE word.

a. Did you sleep .... ?
b. Have you been waiting .... ?
c. I haven't seen her for ....
d. I just stayed .... and took it easy.
e. We only got .... home at twelve.
f. .... have been quite quiet.

Do you remember how these conversations started? Write down the beginnings. Then compare what you wrote with page 46 in the Coursebook.

10 | Good news

Complete the sentences with the words in the box.

best friend	holiday	promoted
birthday	married	visa
exams	place	

1. Hey, guess what? We're getting ....
2. Hey, guess what? I passed all my ....
3. Hey, guess what? I got .... at work.
4. Hey, guess what? It's my .... today.
5. Hey, guess what? I've finally got my .... to go to America.
6. Hey, guess what? I'm going on .... this Friday.
7. Hey, guess what? I've finally found a new .... to live.
8. Hey, guess what? My .... from Greece is coming to visit.

Now match the sentences above with the responses.

1. ☐ 2. ☐ 3. ☐ 4. ☐
5. ☐ 6. ☐ 7. ☐ 8. ☐

a. Oh really? Congratulations! Are you going to get a pay rise as well?
b. Oh really? Congratulations! Did you get good grades?
c. Oh really? That's great! So when're you going to go?
d. Oh really? That's great! Is it a flat or a shared house, or what?
e. Oh really? That's great! Where are you going?
f. Oh really? Congratulations! How old are you – if you don't mind me asking?
g. Oh really? Congratulations! When's the big day?
h. Oh really? That's great! Has she been here before?

7 School and studying

1 Your academic career

Complete the paragraphs with the words in the boxes.

Paragraph 1

degree	graduated	job	Master's

I (1) .... last year and now I'm in the middle of doing a two-year (2) .... in fashion design. I did my (3) .... in art history, but I've always been interested in clothes as well. Also, I think there's more chance of finding a (4) .... as a fashion designer than as an art historian! That's why I decided to do this course.

Paragraph 2

do	primary schools	university
leaves	secondary school	

My daughter is in her fifth year of (5) .... now and she's doing really well. She says she wants to go to (6) .... after she (7) .... and (8) .... French and German. I'm really pleased about it, because when she was young, she went to three different (9) .... We moved around a lot then because of my husband's job and I was worried it would be bad for her.

Paragraph 3

do	go	left	PhD	Master's

I (10) .... school when I was 16 and started working. I was 31 when I finally decided I wanted to (11) .... a degree and (12) .... to university. I enjoyed it so much, I did a (13) .... straight afterwards and now I'm doing my (14) .... It'll be strange to be called Doctor!

2 Conversation

Choose the correct words to complete this conversation.

L: So what do you do, Jane? Are you working or studying or what?

J: I'm (1) .... business management at the London Business School, actually.

L: Oh right. That sounds good. What (2) .... are you in?

J: My third, unfortunately. I've got my (3) .... in the spring. I'm really worried about them.

L: Yes, I can imagine. So what're you going to do when you (4) .... ? Have you decided yet?

J: Yes, I'm going to (5) .... a year off and go travelling a bit and then I'm going to try to get onto a Master's (6) .... somewhere.

L: Oh yes? What in?

J: International finance.

L: Wow. Have you (7) .... anywhere yet?

J: Not yet, but there's a course in Leeds I'm very interested in.

L: Leeds? I've heard it's got a very good reputation. What do you need to do to get in?

J: Well, obviously, I need to get a good grade and then I have to go for (8) ....

L: Oh right. Well, good luck.

J: Thanks. I'll need it. Anyway, Lee, what about you? What do you do?

1.	A making	B doing	C learning	D having
2.	A course	B class	C school	D year
3.	A finals	B tests	C marks	D scores
4.	A pass	B fail	C graduate	D take
5.	A take	B do	C make	D spend
6.	A lesson	B class	C course	D school
7.	A written	B sent	C accepted	D applied
8.	A a talk	B a meeting	C an interview	D a course

Write a conversation between YOU and Lee. For example:

L: So what do you do? Are you working or studying or what?

Y: I'm working in a coffee shop at the moment.

L: …

32

3 Going to

Match the questions with the answers.

1. So what are you going to do when you leave school? ☐

2. So what are you going to do when you graduate? ☐

3. So where are you going to do this course, then? ☐

4. So how are you going to pay your college fees? ☐

a. I'm not really sure yet. I think I might apply to do a Master's somewhere.

b. I'm not really sure yet. I think I might go travelling for a while and then maybe apply to university.

c. I've saved a few thousand pounds over the last three years, so I'll use that.

d. At a college in the north of the city. They run a new course every three months.

Now match these questions with the answers.

5. So what are you going to do if you don't get onto the course? ☐

6. Are you going to that meeting later? ☐

7. Are you going to go away in the summer? ☐

8. What are you going to wear to the party tonight? ☐

e. I'm not really sure yet. I think I might go in these jeans and maybe a different shirt.

f. We're not really sure yet. I think we might go to Morocco for a couple of weeks, if we have enough money.

g. I'm not really sure yet. I suppose I'll try to apply to a few other places, but I hope I won't have to.

h. Yes, of course. I think everyone in the office is going.

4 *Going to* or *might*

Complete the sentences with *going to* or *might* and the verb in brackets.

1. A: What .... you .... after you finish this course? (do)

   B: Well, I've been offered a scholarship to do a PhD in the States, so I .... that in September. (start)

2. A: Have you seen Simon recently?

   B: No, he never goes to lectures. I'm sure he .... all his exams. (fail)

   A: Maybe. I think he .... , though. He is very clever! (pass)

3. A: What .... you .... in the holidays? Are you going away anywhere? (do)

   B: I've missed so many classes, I'm really behind with work. I .... really hard over the holidays and try to catch up. I suppose I .... one day off, but I .... definitely .... on holiday. (study, take, not go)

4. A: What are you doing tonight?

   B: I .... in and finish off my essay. I've got to hand it in tomorrow. Why? (stay)

   A: Oh, I .... Joe Costello in concert and I've got a spare ticket. (see)

   B: Sorry. Try Jeremy. I don't know if he likes Joe Costello, but he .... to go. (want)

Complete each expression from the conversations with ONE word.

a. I've been .... a scholarship

b. Are you going .... anywhere?

c. I'm really .... with work

d. try to .... up

e. I've got a .... ticket

5 Studying at university

Complete the expressions with the verbs in the box.

apply to	give	retake
find	pay back	rewrite

a. .... an essay

b. .... university

c. .... my student loan

d. .... a part-time job

e. .... my exam

f. .... a lecture

Now complete the conversations with the words in the box.

dropped out	lecture	term
essay	started	university
exam	taking	
fell	term	

1. A: Are you going to go to the .... this
      afternoon?
   B: No. I hate the lecturer. She's so boring! I
      .... asleep in the last one
      I went to.

2. A: What's the matter? You're looking stressed out!
   B: I've got an .... this afternoon. I'm
      sure I'm going to fail. I'm terrible at
      .... exams.

3. A: Did you go to .... ?
   B: Yes, I did, but I .... after the first
      year. I just found the course too hard and I was
      too lazy!

4. A: How many weeks are there until the end of
      .... ?
   B: Six more. This .... has been really long!

5. A: When's the deadline for the ....
      we're writing for Mr Jones?
   B: Friday, and I haven't even .... it yet.
      He said we'd get nothing if we hand it in late.

Language note: *teacher, lecturer, professor*

In English, we usually use *teacher* for people who teach
in a *school*. The boss of a school is *the head teacher* or
the head. People who teach at *university* are usually
called *lecturers*. We only use *professor* for someone
who is the head of a university department. You
usually have to publish lots of books and articles
before you can become a *professor*.

6 Could you just ... ?

Match the questions with the follow-up sentences.

1. Sorry, could you just speak up a bit? ☐
2. Sorry, could you just give me a hand with these books? ☐
3. Sorry, could you two just change places? ☐
4. Sorry, could you just be quiet a moment? ☐
5. Sorry, could you just turn the music down a bit? ☐

a. I can't carry them all.
b. So that you're next to someone you haven't spoken to yet.
c. I can't hear you very well.
d. It's really loud and I'm trying to get to sleep!
e. I'm trying to listen to this programme.

Now match these sentences with the follow-up questions.

6. You left the lights on when you went out. ☐
7. You left all your dirty plates on the table after you had dinner. ☐
8. You left the front door unlocked when you left this morning. ☐
9. You left all your things lying around in the front room yesterday. ☐
10. You left the tap running after you had your shower. ☐

f. Could you just make sure you lock it when you go out next time?
g. Could you just wash them up after you've finished?
h. Could you just try to keep things a bit more tidy in future?
i. Could you just make sure you turn them off next time?
j. Could you just make sure you turn it off properly next time?

Language note: *give me a hand*

If you *give someone a hand*, you help them. You can also
ask: *Do you need a hand with those books? Hand* is used
in other expressions in this book. For example, if you
buy a car which someone has used before, you *buy it
second-hand*. If you are *good with your hands*, you're
good at making things. If clothes are *made by hand* or
handmade, then a person made them, not a machine.
Do you have any similar expressions in your language?

7 Key words for writing: *even though* and *although*

Even though and *although* connect something surprising with something that actually happened. For example:

- He lost his job. He was the best teacher.
- He lost his job *even though / although* he was the best teacher.
- *Even though / Although* he was the best teacher he lost his job.

Even though shows it was <u>very</u> surprising. Normally, being the best teacher stops you from losing your job!

Join these sentences using *even though*.

1. I got the job. I didn't have any experience.

2. I got a job in Japan. I didn't speak any Japanese.

3. I didn't study. I passed my exam.

4. I handed in my application form late. They gave me an interview.

5. They're going to move to Italy. They don't speak Italian and they haven't got any work there.

Although is also used to mean 'but'. You don't use *even though* in this situation.

- I'm busy today, but I can meet you tomorrow. *Although* I'm busy today, I can meet you tomorrow.
- I haven't studied French before, but I speak two other languages. *Although* I haven't studied French before, I speak two other languages.

In which sentences can you ONLY use *although*? Cross out even though when you can't use it.

1. I don't have a job at the moment *although / even though* I'm looking for one.
2. He hasn't filled in the application form yet *although / even though* he's had it for weeks.
3. *Even though / Although* I'm terrible at tennis, I enjoy playing.
4. I've never been to the States *although / even though* I'm going on holiday there in the summer.
5. I failed my exam *although / even though* I studied hard.
6. It's quite a boring job, *although / even though* it's close to my house and I can walk there.

8 Writing

Complete this e-mail with the words in the box.

advice	find	shame
at	qualifications	with
experience	quit	

Dear Yago,

Thanks for the card you sent me the other day. We had a really nice time on my birthday. It's a (1) .... you couldn't be there.

I'm actually writing to ask for some (2) .... As you know, I'm working in a shop, but I'm really fed up with it. My boyfriend wants me to (3) .... my job and go to Spain with him to study Spanish. We both need to (4) .... jobs there, though. Do you think it will be possible, even though our Spanish isn't very good? John is very good (5) .... computers and has worked for several internet companies. Obviously, I have lots of (6) .... working in shops, but I don't really want to do that again. I'm quite good with children and I think I would be good (7) .... teaching. The only problem is, I don't have any teaching (8) .... I might do a four-week course to learn how to teach English, though. What do you think? Can you help us?

Terri

Now write a letter to a British, American or Australian friend to ask for some advice about working in their country. Tell them what experience you have, what qualifications you have, what you're good at/with and what you're interested in doing.

8 Work and jobs

1 Questions and answers

Match the questions with the answers.

1. Are you working or studying or what? ☐
2. And what are the hours like? ☐
3. Do you enjoy it? ☐
4. Do you have to work weekends? ☐
5. And do you get much holiday? ☐

a. Apart from the hours, it's great. It's what I've always wanted to do.
b. I'm still at university, although I work part-time in a shop.
c. Yes, that's the best thing about the job! I get about eight weeks a year.
d. Not too bad. I usually finish about five or six and I usually start at half nine.
e. Yes, once every two weeks I work on a Saturday and once a month I have to work on Sunday as well.

Now match these questions with the answers.

6. And do you have to travel very far to work? ☐
7. And what's the money like? Is it OK? ☐
8. How long have you been doing that? ☐
9. What are the other people you work with like? ☐
10. So what about you? What do you do? ☐

f. About five years now.
g. Nothing at the moment. I'm unemployed.
h. It's OK, but it's not brilliant. Hopefully, I'll get a pay rise soon.
i. No. I'm really lucky because it's only five minutes' walk from my house.
j. They're great. We get on really well.

Language note: *apart from*

We use *apart from* to show that one thing is different from everything else. For example:
Everyone at work is British, apart from me. I'm French.
Apart from the weather, Britain is a great place to live.
It's a really good school, apart from the fact they don't have any computers.
I love my job, apart from the fact the money's not very good.

2 Conversation

Complete this conversation with questions. Look at Exercise 1 to help you, if you need to.

J: So what do you do, Nori? (1) .... ?

N: Well, I graduated a couple of years ago and now I'm working in Osaka.

J: Oh right. So (2) .... ?

N: I'm a civil servant. I work for the government.

J: Oh, do you? (3) .... ?

N: Yes, it's OK. I have to do a lot of paperwork, which is quite boring, but it's quite well-paid.

J: Oh, that sounds good.

N: Yes, it is, but sometimes I get a bit bored with it. I have to work a twelve-hour day most days. A lot of the time, I don't really have much to do, so I just sit around and kill time.

J: (4) .... ?

N: No, thank goodness! Five days a week is enough.

J: Yes, I know what you mean. (5) .... ?

N: It's not too bad. I get three weeks a year, so that's OK.

J: And (6) .... ?

N: Yes, quite a long way. It's about an hour on the train, so I have to spend a lot of time commuting. Anyway, (7) .... , Jenny? What do you do?

3 Do you enjoy your job?

Complete the answers to the question above with *have to* or *don't have to*.

1. I hate it. I .... go to so many boring meetings. I can't stand it.
2. It's great. I .... work very hard.
3. It's great. I mean, I .... wear a suit and tie to the office. I can just wear what I like.
4. It's great, apart from the fact that I .... wear a horrible uniform. I look really stupid in it.
5. It's OK. I work quite hard, but I .... take work home with me, which is good.
6. Yes, it's great. I .... start work until ten.

4 | I have to …

Match the statements with the reasons.

1. I have to go to a meeting about the new computer system.
2. I have to pass these exams.
3. I have to practise my English.
4. I have to get a visa.
5. I have to do the shopping.
6. I have to be outside the hotel by nine.

a. I won't be able to go if I don't.
b. I won't get better if I don't.
c. I won't be able to use it if I don't.
d. The coach will leave without me if I'm not there.
e. I won't get into university if I don't.
f. We won't have anything to eat if I don't.

5 | Jobs

Complete the lists with the words in the box.

designer	guard	manager
driver	instructor	

1. graphic .... / interior .... / fashion .... / web ....

2. driving .... / ski .... / flying .... / swimming ....

3. assistant .... / marketing .... / sales .... / office ....

4. bus .... / lorry .... / train .... / taxi ....

5. life........................... / security .... / body........................... / prison ....

6 | Compound nouns

All the jobs in Exercise 5 are examples of compound nouns. In English, we often put two nouns together to make a new word. In many languages you do this by using the word *of* or *for*. For example:

- We say *bus driver* NOT ~~driver of bus~~.
- We say *the school bus* NOT ~~the bus for school children~~.

The second noun is the thing we are talking about and the first noun is like an adjective. The first noun is never in the plural. For example:

- We say *bus drivers* NOT ~~buses~~ drivers.

Nouns that are used as adjectives often go with lots of nouns. For example:

bus station   *bus ticket*   *bus stop*   *bus lane*   *bus route*

Complete the lists with the words in the box.

alarm	book	car	football	ticket

1. a .... shirt / a .... match / a .... stadium / my .... boots

2. a train .... / a .... machine / a return .... / the .... office

3. a history .... / a .... shop / a .... shelf / a text ....

4. an .... clock / a fire .... / a burglar .... / a car ....

5. a .... park / a sports .... / a .... crash / a .... mechanic

Now complete the sentences with compound nouns from the lists above.

a. We saw a really nasty .... on the way here. I hope no-one was killed.

b. We all had to leave the building because the .... went off.

c. I gave my girlfriend a Leeds United .... , but she never wears it!

d. If you don't want to queue up, you can use the .... at the entrance to the station.

e. I paid £300 for the course, but I still had to buy the .... we used in class!

f. I work as a .... for a local taxi company.

g. Could you put the dictionary back on the .... when you've finished with it?

h. I live in a block of flats next to a .... I can see the pitch from my bedroom window.

7 | My job

Complete the paragraphs with the words in the boxes.

Paragraph 1

days off	easy	little	take
earn	flexible	sacked	times

I became a taxi driver after I got (1) .... from my job as security guard. Being a taxi driver is a good job because it's very (2) .... I can start and finish when I want because people need taxis at all (3) .... of the day and night. I usually work evenings and nights because you can (4) .... more money then, especially on Fridays and Saturdays. I usually (5) .... Mondays and Tuesdays off. On my (6) .... I usually just take it (7) .... and do as (8) .... as possible!

Paragraph 2

afternoons	get	leave	over
college	hours	novel	published

I teach English as a foreign language in a (9) .... in England. Apart from the fact I have to (10) .... for work at seven in the morning, I love my job. I (11) .... to meet lots of really interesting people from all (12) .... the world. Even though I have to get up early, the (13) .... are actually really good. I finish teaching at twelve o'clock, so I have the (14) .... free. I spend my afternoons going to the cinema, and reading and writing books. My first book was (15) .... this year. It's a (16) .... about a teacher of English who falls in love with one of her students.

Paragraph 3

all	dying	long	stressful
apart from	equipment	paperwork	well-paid

I'm a doctor. (17) .... the money, I hate my job. I have to work really (18) .... hours and it's very (19) .... You're with sick people (20) .... day. You have to tell people they're (21) .... or their relatives have died. You have to do lots of (22) .... – everything you do has to be written down and explained. Sometimes we don't have the (23) .... or drugs to help patients. It's really terrible. I only do the job because it's quite (24) .... , and I have to look after my wife and seven children.

8 Present perfect

Write present perfect questions using the verbs in brackets.

1. .... you .... to our country before? (be)

2. .... you .... round Europe much? (travel)

3. .... you .... any good films recently? (see)

4. .... you .... the new Bobby Zamora CD? (hear)

5. .... you .... much experience of this kind of work? (have)

6. .... you .... anything for it? (take)

7. .... you .... this game before? (play)

8. .... you ever .... snake? (eat)

Now match the answers with the questions above.

1. ☐   2. ☐   3. ☐   4. ☐
5. ☐   6. ☐   7. ☐   8. ☐

a. Not really. I've been to Spain and I went to Paris for a weekend last year, but that's about it.

b. Yes, it's brilliant, isn't it? I love the last song. I play it all the time.

c. No, this is my first time here.

d. No, not at all. This is my first job!

e. No, never. What does it taste like?

f. No, not really. I went to see *Dogs of War* a few weeks ago, but it was rubbish!

g. No, I'll be all right. I just need to take it easy.

h. No, but I'm sure you can teach me. I'm a quick learner.

Complete each expression from the sentences with ONE word.

i. but that's .... it

j. What does it taste .... ?

k. that film was ....

l. take it ....

m. I'm a .... learner.

9 Vocabulary: getting a job

Complete the conversations with the pairs of words in the box.

an application form + details
an interview + brilliant
fill in + company
interested + the job
offer + start
the interview + hope
the job + celebrate
thing + office work

1. A: I'm looking for a job at the moment.
   B: Oh, yes? What kind of .... ?
   A: Just ....

2. A: There was a job in the paper this morning that you might be .... in.
   B: Oh, yes? What was .... ?
   A: It was for an admin assistant in a college.

3. A: Hello, I'd like .... for the job you advertised in The Mail this morning.
   B: Yes, of course. Can I take your .... ?
   A: Sure. The name's Harry Smith and the address is 102 Fairford Road, Swindon.

4. A: I'm sorry, I can't come tonight. I've got to stay in and .... an application form.
   B: Oh right, OK. So what's it for?
   A: It's for a job in an electronics ....

5. A: I've got .... for that job I applied for. It's next week.
   B: That's .... When is it exactly?
   A: Thursday morning.

6. A: Good luck with .... tomorrow. I .... you get it.
   B: Yes, me too. Thanks.
   A: Well, I'll keep my fingers crossed.

7. A: We'd like to .... you the job, if you're still interested.
   B: Yes, definitely. That's brilliant. When do you want me to .... ?
   A: As soon as possible.

8. A: Hey, guess what? I got .... !
   B: Congratulations. Are you going to go out and .... ?
   A: Yes, I'm going to go for a drink later, if you'd like to come.

9 | Eating out

1 | What was the restaurant like?

Complete the answers to the above question with the words in the box.

choice	food	portions	waiters
empty	full	spicy	

1. I didn't really like it. All the food was too
   .... I don't like chilli and hot food.

2. The food was really nice, but the ....
   were too small. I was still hungry when I finished.

3. It was OK, but there wasn't much ....
   They didn't even have a vegetarian option.

4. It was nice, but the portions are almost too big. I was
   .... after the first course!

5. It was great. The .... was delicious and the
   .... were really friendly and efficient.

6. The food was really nice, but the place was almost
   .... , which was a shame.

2 | There's a nice place …

Complete the sentences with the words in the box.

Greek Street	me	quite a lot	seafood

1. There's a nice place on the sea-front, which does
   really good ....

2. There's a nice Italian place in Camden, which we go
   to ....

3. There's a really good fish place on ....

4. There's a really good Thai place near ....

Now complete these sentences with the words in the box.

a buffet for lunch	outside	quite cheap	work

5. There's a really good vegetarian restaurant round the
   corner from ....

6. There's a Chinese place down the road which is
   ....

7. There's a nice place just across the road which does
   ....

8. There's a nice place near here where you can sit
   ....

3 | Conversation

Complete the conversation with ONE word in each space.

M: Are you hungry?

K: Yes, (1) .... bit.

M: Do you want to (2) .... something to eat,
then?

K: Yes, OK. Have you got anywhere in (3) .... ?

M: Well, there's a really nice pizza place just round the
(4) ....

K: Well, actually, I went (5) .... a pizza last
night. I don't really feel (6) .... another
one. Do you know anywhere (7) .... ?

M: Well, there's a really nice Thai place
(8) .... Soho.

K: Right. Is it very spicy? I don't really
(9) .... very hot food.

M: No, it's not too bad. They've got (10) ....
of dishes to choose from. Honestly, it's really nice
food. I'm (11) .... you'll like it.

K: OK then, I'll try (12) .... once.

M: (13) .... we walk or do you want to
get the bus?

K: I don't mind. It's (14) .... to you.

**Can you remember where the pauses and the
stressed sounds are in this conversation? Mark
the pauses // and <u>underline</u> the stressed syllables.
For example:**

M: Are you <u>hung</u>ry?
K: <u>Yes</u> // a <u>bit</u>.

**Compare your ideas about the pauses and
stressed sounds with the tapescript in the
Coursebook.**

**Write a conversation between YOU and Mel. Use
some of the ideas in Exercise 2 to help you
decide where to eat.**

4 Refusing food and drink

Put the words in order and make sentences.

1. full / really / I'm

   ....

2. drink / don't / I

   ....

3. diet / on / I'm / a

   ....

4. mustn't / more / any / have / I

   ....

5. anything / really / don't / I / spicy / like

   ....

6. sweet / I / don't / like / anything / really

   ....

7. one / just / I've / had

   ....

8. sleep / won't / to / be / I / able

   ....

9. another / I / thing / eat / couldn't

   ....

Translate the sentences above into your language.

1. ....
2. ....
3. ....
4. ....
5. ....
6. ....
7. ....
8. ....
9. ....

Test yourself. Spend five minutes memorising the sentences. Then cover the sentences and write as much as you can remember on a piece of paper. Use your translations to help you. How much did you get right?

5 *Some* and *any*

Complete the sentences with *some* or *any*.

1. A: Do you like Grant Archer?

   B: I quite like .... of his books, but .... of them are rubbish.

2. A: What kind of music do you like?

   B: ....thing really. I don't have .... special preferences.

3. A: Have you got .... brothers or sisters?

   B: No, it's just me. I'm an only child.

4. A: Can I borrow some money? The cash machine's not giving .... out.

   B: Sorry, I haven't got much on me. Ask Yuka. She might be able to lend you ....

5. A: I'm sorry, but does the lasagne have cheese in it? I'm not allowed to eat .... dairy products. I'm allergic to them.

   B: Not much, but it does have .... on top. How about the spaghetti? That doesn't have ....

6. Be careful when you eat the fish. There might be .... bones still in it, although I've tried to get rid of most of them.

7. I really shouldn't be eating .... chocolate or things like that at the moment because I'm trying to lose .... weight. But I suppose one small piece won't hurt!

8. A: We should go out for a meal ....time.

   B: Yes, definitely. I can go .... day next week. I don't have .... plans at the moment.

   A: OK. Well, how about Thursday?

   B: Great. I'll give you a ring early next week.

Language note: *get rid of*

When you're cooking fish, it's nice if you *try to get rid of all the bones* before you serve it. When you move house, sometimes you *have to get rid of some of your furniture* – maybe you sell it or you give it away, or you just throw it away. Sometimes, in the winter, you *can't get rid of your cold*.

41

6 Irregular past simple

Complete the paragraphs with the past simple form of the verbs. All the verbs are irregular.

1. It was really embarrassing. I was in class once and I
   .... down to write something on the
   board and I .... my trousers. (bend, tear)

2. I was walking along and I stepped on a banana skin,
   and I slipped and .... I ....
   really stupid. (fall, feel)

3. I borrowed my brother's mobile phone once and I
   dropped it and it .... I .... to
   buy him a new one and it .... me £200.
   He didn't let me borrow it again! (break, have, cost)

4. I .... to a friend's party and his mother
   had made a big chocolate cake. I .... four
   or five slices and then I .... really, really
   sick. (go, eat, feel)

5. One day, I .... a letter to my parents and
   another one to my girlfriend. Unfortunately, I
   .... the letters in the wrong envelope and
   .... them to the wrong people. My
   parents .... the letter to my girlfriend up
   when they .... it – and ....
   me I shouldn't be writing those kinds of things!
   (write, put, send, tear, see, tell)

7 Restaurant vocabulary

Match the questions with the replies.

1. Could I have some water? ☐
2. Would you like to see the dessert menu? ☐
3. Could we book a table for six at nine o'clock? ☐
4. I'm afraid the beef is off the menu. ☐
5. Do we need to leave a tip? ☐
6. Sorry, but I ordered chicken noodles, not beef. ☐
7. Have you got a cloth? I've just spilt some water. ☐
8. Would you like a high chair for the little boy? ☐

a. No thanks. Could you just bring the bill?
b. Oh right. Well, in that case, I'll have the chicken.
c. No, it's OK. Service is included.
d. Certainly sir. I'll just go and get one.
e. Certainly. Still or sparkling?
f. That'd be great. Thanks. She's a girl, though!
g. I'm terribly sorry. Would you like me to change that?
h. I'm terribly sorry, but we're completely full tonight.

8 Food: ways of cooking

Look at the pictures. Find the ways of cooking.

chopped ☐   grilled ☐
boiled ☐   roasted ☐
fried ☐   mashed ☐
squeezed ☐   steamed ☐
toasted ☐   sliced ☐

A 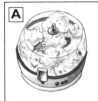 **B** **C**

D  **E** **F**

G **H**  **I**

J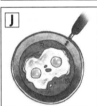

Cover the words above and complete the dishes on the menu.

1. T................................. bread covered with c.................................
   tomatoes and crushed garlic.

2. S................................. sea bass on a bed of r.................................
   peppers.

3. G................................. sausages with m.................................
   potato.

4. Steak served with a choice of b................................. new
   potatoes or chips.

5. Freshly s................................. orange juice.

6. Freshly s................................. mango.

9 | Key words for writing: *then* and *so*

We use *so* to show the result of something:

- The restaurant was fully booked, *so* we went to McDonald's

We also use *so* to show the reason for doing something:

- Turn down the heat on the cooker *so* it doesn't burn.

We use *then* to show the order of actions: *First, ... Then ... ,* and *then ... . Finally, ...* . We start a new sentence with *Then*. If you don't want to start a new sentence, you need to say *and then*. For example:

- First of all they got our order wrong. *Then* they overcharged us.
- Chop the onions, garlic and chilli into very small pieces. *Then* fry them in some olive oil.
- Cook the onions for ten minutes *and then* add the other vegetables.

Complete the sentences with *so*, *then* or *and then*.

1. There was quite a long queue at the cinema, ... we had to wait for over half an hour.

2. We had a really nice meal .... we went for a walk by the river.

3. I had a really big first course, ... I didn't have a dessert.

4. Heat the oil first. .... put the vegetables in the pan.

5. I burnt the dinner, ... we had to ring and get a take-away pizza.

6. We had soup for the first course. .... we had a really nice fish dish .... we had lamb, and after that I think we had two more courses. I was so full when we finished!

7. Cook the garlic slowly .... it tastes nice and sweet.

8. Taste the sauce .... add some more salt and pepper, if necessary.

Language note: *after that*

You can use *after that* or *next* instead of *then*. For example:
We went for a meal at a restaurant near here and after that we went into town.

10 | Writing: recipes

Last night, Harry cooked dinner for Josie. This morning, she has sent him a thank-you e-mail. Complete Harry's reply with the words in the box.

after	and then	finally	first	so	then	until	while

Dear Josie,

I'm glad you liked the food. Here's the recipe you asked for. It's from a great book called Real Fast Food by Nigel Slater. For four people you need: 2 onions, 2 or 3 cloves of garlic, 2 fresh green chillies, 8 tomatoes, 4 medium red peppers, 4 eggs, salt and pepper, fresh herbs.

(1) .... of all, slice the onions and garlic thinly and fry them slowly for 10 to 15 minutes so they become nice and sweet.
(2) .... the onions are cooking, take the seeds out of the chillies and the red peppers, and then chop them up. Chop the tomatoes as well, (3) .... add these vegetables to the onions and stir well, adding salt and pepper. Leave everything to cook slowly. You might need to add some water
(4) .... it doesn't stick to the pan, and cover it, if you have a lid which is big enough. (5) .... about 10 or 15 minutes, the mixture should be soft with a little liquid. Make four small holes in the mixture for the eggs. (6) .... break the eggs and drop them carefully in the holes without breaking them. Continue cooking
(7) .... the eggs are done and then turn off the heat.
(8) .... , chop some fresh herbs and throw them on the top. That's it!

I'll give you a ring again soon.

Harry

Now write an e-mail to a friend who wants to know a recipe for something YOU cooked.

10 Family

1 Questions we ask about families

Match the questions with the answers.

1. Have you got any brothers or sisters? ☐
2. How old are they? ☐
3. What're they like? Do you get on? ☐
4. What do your parents do? ☐
5. Are you married? ☐
6. Have you got any kids? ☐
7. Are your grandparents still alive? ☐
8. Have you got a boyfriend? ☐

a. Yes, we've got two – a boy and a girl.
b. My mum's a housewife and my dad runs his own business.
c. My older brother is twenty-six and my little brother's eleven.
d. Only one of them is – my gran on my mum's side. The other three have all passed away.
e. No, I'm single, actually.
f. Yes. We live together, actually.
g. Yes, we get on quite well, but I'm closer to my older brother than I am to my younger one.
h. Yes, two brothers. One older, one younger.

Language note: *on my mum's side*

My grandparents *on my mum's side* are my mother's parents. We also talk about *my dad's side of the family*. For example:
Quite a few people on my father's side of the family are doctors.
I've got lots of relatives on my dad's side who live in the States.
I've never met a lot of my relatives on my mother's side.

2 Married

Complete the sentences with the words in the box.

divorce	immediate	registry office
engaged	marry	separated
extended	reception	the big day
get married		

1. A: Hey, guess what? Jim proposed to me on Friday – and I accepted, so we're .... now!
   B: Oh really? Well, congratulations! When's .... ?

2. My boyfriend asked me to .... him last month, but I turned him down. I'm not ready for marriage yet!

3. My girlfriend and I are engaged. We're going to .... next year.

4. We had a huge wedding. We had all of our .... families. I met cousins I didn't even know I had! On top of that, we invited all our friends and all the people we worked with.

5. We had quite a big wedding. We had about 80 guests at our ....

6. Unfortunately, my wife and I are .... and our three kids live with her. She has a new boyfriend now and wants us to get a ....

7. We only had a small wedding – we just invited our .... families and a few close friends.

8. We got married in a .... because neither of us is very religious.

3 Conversation

Complete the conversation with the words in brackets in the correct form.

M: What (1) .... (you / do) after the class? Have you got time for a coffee?

S: No, I've got to go. I (2) .... (go round) to my sister's for dinner. She gets a bit annoyed if I'm late.

M: Oh right. Where (3) .... (she / live)?

S: Pinedo.

M: Right, that's a nice part of town. What (4) .... (she / do)?

S: She's a doctor. She (5) .... (work) in the Central Hospital.

M: Oh, OK. So how old is she? She must be a lot (6) .... (old) than you.

S: Yes, she's 35 years old, so she's almost 15 years (7) .... (old) than me.

M: Wow. That's quite a big age gap. So what's she like? Do you get on?

S: Yes, she's really nice. We're actually quite similar. She's probably a bit (8) .... (organised) than I am, but she's quite funny and very easy to talk to. You know, she's never treated me like a baby or her little sister.

M: That's good. So is she married?

S: Yes, she got married when she was really young. I think they (9) .... (be married) for around twelve years. It wasn't long after they graduated.

M: OK, so have they got any kids?

S: She's actually pregnant at the moment. It's her first baby.

M: Really? That's great. When's it due?

S: November.

M: Oh right. It's quite soon then.

S: Yes, it's quite exciting. It (10) .... (be) my first time as an aunt. Anyway, what about you? Have you got any brothers or sisters?

4 Describing what people are like

Complete the descriptions with the sentences in the box.

He's a bit shy.	She's a bit quiet.
He's really nice.	She's really fit.
He's very generous.	She's very funny.
He's very honest.	She's very relaxed.

1. .... She always makes me laugh.

2. .... He's not very good at talking to people he doesn't know.

3. .... He's a really lovely, friendly person.

4. .... He bought everyone a drink after work the other day.

5. .... She doesn't really say very much.

6. .... He always tells the truth.

7. .... She doesn't really worry about things.

8. .... She does a lot of exercise and plays a lot of sport.

Now match these sentences with the opposites above.

1. ☐ 2. ☐ 3. ☐ 4. ☐
5. ☐ 6. ☐ 7. ☐ 8. ☐

a. She's very talkative, very chatty.

b. He's horrible. He's a really nasty person.

c. She's quite unfit.

d. He's a liar. You can't trust him at all.

e. She's quite a tense person. She worries too much!

f. She's got no sense of humour at all!

g. He's very sociable, very out-going.

h. He's really mean.

Language note: *fit* and *healthy*

You *keep fit* by doing lots of exercise. If you're very *unfit*, you get out of breath walking up the stairs because you do little exercise. You're *healthy* if you eat the right kinds of food and you don't get ill. You can have a *healthy diet* with lots of fruit and vegetables, and a *healthy lifestyle* when you don't drink or smoke.

5 Comparatives

Complete the sentences with the comparative form of the adjectives in the box.

hard-working   old   quiet   tall   young

1. My oldest sister is almost twenty years .... than me.

2. My sister is a bit .... than I am. She works weekends and she works late most days. I'm too lazy to do that kind of thing!

3. Sometimes, I find it quite hard to talk to my brother. He's quite shy. He's much .... than me.

4. My younger brother is already ten centimetres .... than me – and he's only 15. He's going to be huge when he's older!

5. My little sister is eight years .... than me.

Now complete these sentences with the comparative form of the adjectives in the box.

fit   lazy   open   relaxed   serious

6. My dad worries all the time about his business and about his children, but my mum doesn't really worry about anything! My mum is a lot .... than my dad.

7. My dad goes running three times a week, he plays tennis a lot and he cycles to work every day! It's embarrassing to say, but I think he's probably a bit .... than I am.

8. My older brother is .... than my big sister. She's really hard-working, but he's unemployed at the moment – and is too lazy to find a job.

9. It's strange, but my gran is a lot .... than my mum is. I can talk to my gran about almost anything, but my mum doesn't really like talking about her feelings.

10. My sister likes going out and partying and making new friends, but I'm more interested in my studies and my future career. I suppose I'm just a bit .... than my sister

Complete each expression from the sentences with ONE word.

a. I .... it quite hard to talk to him

b. worries .... the time.

c. .... running

d. cycles to ....

e. my future ....

6 My family

Choose the correct words to complete this paragraph.

My parents got (1) .... in 1969, but it didn't work out for them. They got (2) .... when I was nine or ten, and my brother and I then went to live with my mum. My dad had been married once before that and had a daughter from his first (3) .... – my (4) .... , June, but I don't really know her very well. I think she lives in Zimbabwe. Anyway, when I was 14 or 15, my dad got (5) .... and he's still with Mel, my (6) .... She also has a daughter from her first marriage – Polly, my (7) .... My brother is three years younger than me, and he and his wife have a daughter, Moira, my (8) .... My mum also has a new (9) .... , John, but they have decided they don't want to get married. As for me, well, I'm (10) .... to my lovely fiancée, Lucy, and we're getting married next summer. I'm really looking forward to it.

1. A met	B in love	C married	D marry
2. A divorced	B split up	C finished	D over
3. A love	B marry	C time	D marriage
4. A half-sister	B sister	C step-sister	D cousin
5. A remarried	B together	C marry	D in love
6. A half-mother	B aunt	C step-mother	D mother
7. A half-sister	B sister	C step-sister	D cousin
8. A niece	B aunt	C step-daughter	D nephew
9. A husband	B friend	C partner	D fiancé
10. A separated	B married	C live together	D engaged

7 Collocations

Match the sentence beginnings and endings.

1. We're thinking of moving ☐
2. I'm thinking of changing ☐
3. My parents are going to get ☐
4. My son is going to leave ☐
5. My gran might need to move ☐
6. My boyfriend and I might get ☐

a. into an old people's home, if she doesn't get any better.

b. my career. I'm bored with teaching. I'd like to retrain.

c. married next year – if my parents say it's OK.

d. house next year, if we can afford it.

e. home in the autumn, when he starts university.

f. divorced. They told me last week!

8 Expressions with *friend*

Complete the sentences with the expressions in the box.

> a few close friends
> a friend of a friend
> is it OK if I bring a friend
> just good friends
> made any friends
> my friend from Peru
> my friends from university

1. A: So Tom, is it true that you and Jan are going out together?
   B: No! Who told you that? We're ....

2. A: So how do you know Luke?
   B: Oh, I don't really know him very well, actually. He's .... , really.

3. A: Are you still coming to our wedding reception next Saturday?
   B: Yes, of course, but I wanted to ask you – .... ?
   A: Yes, of course. Why not?

4. I'm thinking of joining this website I read about. You can get back in touch with people you used to know. I've lost touch with most of .... and would love to meet some of them again.

5. It's hard for me here. I get quite lonely sometimes. I haven't really .... since I arrived here last spring.

6. A: Oh, Dawn. I'd like you to meet Ralph, ...
   B: Oh, hello, Ralph. Nice to meet you. Is this your first time here in London?

7. A: So how many people are coming to the wedding?
   B: Not many. Just our family and ....

Language note: *died* and *dead*

Died is the past simple form of the verb *die*. *Dead* is an adjective which we use with the verb *be*. We say *my grandparents are dead*, but *my grandmother died last year*. Other things can be described as *dead*. For example:
The battery's dead. I need to recharge it.
The area's dead – there's nothing to do.

9 Died of / died in

Complete the sentences with the words in the box.

> age   AIDS   cancer   overdose   sleep   war

1. Over two million people died in the civil .... between the north and the south in our country.

2. Some people think Marilyn Monroe didn't die of a drugs .... They think she was murdered.

3. My father died of lung .... He smoked all his life.

4. My grandfather was really unhealthy – he smoked, he drank, he ate too much – but he still lived to be 96 and died in his .... of old ....

5. It's terrible. Millions of people are dying of .... round the world because people are too embarrassed to talk about HIV and how they can avoid getting infected.

10 The internet and computers

Complete the sentences with the words in the box.

> answer   download   on-line
> check   go   receive
> crashed   member   sent
> damage

1. I often .... music from the internet and make my own compilation CDs.

2. It's often cheaper to book flights ....

3. A: Don't you ever .... your e-mails at home? I've .... you lots, but you never .... !
   B: I'm sorry. I .... so many at work, the last thing I want to do is look through my e-mails at home as well.

4. A: I think there was a virus in that e-mail you sent me yesterday.
   B: Oh no, really? Did it do much .... ?
   A: No, not really. I mean, the computer .... when I opened the attachment, but I started it up again and it seemed to be OK after that.

5. A: What do you do when you're on the internet all night?
   B: I mainly just .... to different chat rooms and chat to people. I'm also a .... of various on-line news groups.

1 Around town

Complete the sentences with the words in the box.

bridge	junction	roundabout	stadium
church	lights	signs	subway
crossing	monument		

1. It's a very busy road, but there's a .... which goes under it to the other side.

2. Let's not cross the road here. There's too much traffic. There's a .... just down there.

3. There's a big .... in the main square commemorating our country's independence.

4. Go straight on through the traffic .... until you get to a Catholic ....

5. If you're coming south on the motorway, you're best coming off at .... 6 and then follow the .... to Little Hampton.

6. Keep going until you get to the river. Don't go over the .... , but turn left along the river.

7. Keep going until you get to a .... Then go all the way round and take the fourth exit.

8. We live next to a sports .... , so it's very noisy when there's a match on.

2 Verbs for giving directions

Match the sentence beginnings with the endings.

1. Go under ☐ a. going straight on.

2. Keep ☐ b. the first turning on your right.

3. Take ☐ c. that road on your right.

4. It's along ☐ d. the subway to cross the road from the car park.

5. You can't ☐ e. miss it

6. Come off ☐ f. the third house along that road.

7. Follow ☐ g. the motorway at junction 12.

8. We're ☐ h. the signs to Maldon.

1 Conversation

Complete the conversation with ONE word in each space.

T: Excuse me, could you help me?

P: Sorry?

T: Do you (1) .... if this is the (2) .... to The Gagosian?

P: I'm sorry. What's that?

T: The Gagosian. It's an art gallery.

P: I've no (3) ....

T: Sorry?

P: I'm sorry. I'm not from (4) .... here myself. I don't really know the (5) .... Ask this guy here. Hey, excuse me, mate.

L: Yes?

P: Do you know a place round here called ... Sorry, what was it called (6) .... ?

T: The Gagosian.

P: It's a gallery.

L: Oh right. Yes, I think I know the (7) .... It's down there (8) .... Down past the park, but I'm not (9) .... whereabouts exactly.

T: Sorry?

L: I'm not sure where it is exactly, but it's down there somewhere. (10) .... the signs to Hall Green. Just keep going (11) .... on down this road, straight on (12) .... you get to a park. It's around (13) .... somewhere. Ask someone else when you (14) .... there.

T: OK. Thank you very much.

L: No problem. I (15) .... you find it.

Write a conversation between YOU and a local when you are visiting an area you don't know and looking for a place.

4 You're best ...-ing

We often give advice with the structure *you're best* + *-ing*. For example:

- If you're coming south on the motorway, *you're best coming* off at junction 6.
- It's miles away. *You're best taking* a bus.

Complete the sentences with the words in the box.

e-mailing	going to
getting a taxi	taking the bus
getting the train	taking the underground
going by coach	talking to

1. A: How do I get to your house from the centre of town?
   B: You're best .... The number 23 more or less goes past our house.

2. A: How can I get to Oxford from here?
   B: You're best .... It's cheaper than the train and it's direct. There's no direct train.

3. A: How do I get into town from here?
   B: You're best .... There's a tube station just round the corner.

4. A: How do I get to the hotel from here?
   B: You're best .... There isn't a bus or train that goes there directly and it's too far to walk.

5. A: How do I get to Windsor from here?
   B: You're best .... There's a service which goes from Paddington Station every 15 minutes.

6. A: How can I get in contact with you?
   B: You're best .... me. I check it quite often.

7. A: Where can I get a good guidebook?
   B: You're best .... Dyson's, the bookshop in Tyler Street. They've got a huge travel section.

8. A: How can I improve my English?
   B: You're best just .... people and practising it as much as possible.

Do you agree with the final piece of advice about improving your English? Write your own idea here.

You're best ....

5 Indirect questions

We often start questions with *Could you tell me*. These follow the same pattern as *Do you know ... ?* questions. We ask *Could you tell me ... ?* questions when we think the person should know the answer. We use these structures a lot because the questions sound more polite.

Rewrite these questions with *Could you tell me*.

1. Where's the toilet?
   ....

2. What time does the class start?
   ....

3. What stop do I need to get off at?
   ....

4. How much are the tickets?
   ....

5. Are there any places left on the course?
   ....

6. How long does the course last?
   ....

7. Are the coursebooks included in the fees?
   ....

8. Who do I need to speak to about the course?
   ....

6 Can / could

Complete the sentences with *can, can't, could,* or *couldn't*.

1. I .... drive. I've had three glasses of wine.

2. The train was so packed I .... get on.

3. I had to wait for three buses to go past before I .... get one.

4. You .... get there by car or train because of the mountains. You have to fly there.

5. You .... get a tram out to the airport now. They finished building the line there last year.

6. Sorry I'm late. I .... find anywhere to park.

7. The road was blocked off, so you .... only get through on foot.

8. Why don't we cycle there? You .... borrow my brother's bike.

9. You .... smoke on any international flights now.

7 Travel compound nouns

Complete the compound nouns with the words in the box. Then translate the compound nouns into your language.

card	jam	parks	road	works

1. traffic ....
2. travel ....
3. road........................... ....
4. main ....
5. car ....

Complete these compound nouns with the words in the box. Then translate them.

hour	insurance	street	system	ticket

6. transport ....
7. rush ....
8. car ....
9. return ....
10. side ....

Complete the sentences with compound nouns.

11. You don't need to use your car in our city because it has a really good .... It's very cheap and very reliable.

12. It's not a very nice place to live. It's really noisy and polluted because our flat's on a big ....

13. Although we live in the city centre, the noise isn't too bad because our flat is on a quiet ....

14. I'm thinking of selling my car because it's so expensive. My .... went up again this year. I have to pay almost £600 a year now.

15. There are a lot of problems with parking in the area, so they're building two new underground ....

16. Sorry we're late. There were .... on the motorway, so the traffic was moving very slowly.

17. Sorry we're so late. There was an awful accident on the motorway.
I think six or seven cars were involved and it caused a big .... while they were clearing the road.

18. I'm thinking of taking the train to work instead of driving. A weekly .... costs about the same as parking in the city centre.

8 Travel conversations

Put the sentences in order and make conversations.

Conversation 1: on the bus

a. Yes.
b. Could you tell me when I have to get off?
c. Is this the right bus for Fleetwood?
d. No problem. Take a seat.

1. ☐ 2. ☐ 3. ☐ 4. ☐

Conversation 2: at the ticket office

a. OK. That'll be £35, please.
b. No, I'm coming back on Thursday.
c. Are you returning today?
d. I'd like a return ticket to Bath, please.

1. ☐ 2. ☐ 3. ☐ 4. ☐

Conversation 3: at the train station

a. Platform three.
b. You need to go over the footbridge at the end of this platform.
c. I'm sorry. Could you tell me which platform I need for Edinburgh?
d. OK. Thanks. Where is it?

1. ☐ 2. ☐ 3. ☐ 4. ☐

Conversation 4: at the train information desk

a. 10.24.
b. Could you tell me when the last train back to Nottingham is?
c. 11.13.
d. And what time does it get in?

1. ☐ 2. ☐ 3. ☐ 4. ☐

Conversation 5: in a taxi

a. £17, please.
b. This is the road. Could you just pull over when you can?
c. Yeah, that's fine. How much is it?
d. OK. Could I have a receipt?
e. Sure. Is just here OK?
f. Thanks. Bye.
g. Sure, here you go. And your change.

1. ☐ 2. ☐ 3. ☐ 4. ☐
5. ☐ 6. ☐ 7. ☐ 8. ☐

9 Key words for writing: *when* and *until*

***When* shows the time an action is happening or starts:**

- *When* you get to the traffic lights, turn left.
- I came to university *when* I was 29, so I've got two more years before I graduate.
- I broke my leg *when* I was at school.

***Until* shows the time an action stops:**

- Keep going straight on *until* you get to the traffic lights. Then turn left.
- I studied at university *until* I was 29, so I've only been working for two years.

***Until* often goes with negatives:**

- She didn't have her first baby *until* she was 43.
- I didn't get home from work *until* ten o'clock last night.

Complete the sentences with *when* or *until*.

1. Go straight on and keep going .... you get to a big roundabout with a statue in the middle.

2. .... you come out of the building, turn right.

3. Give me a ring .... you get to the airport and I'll come and pick you up.

4. Stay on the motorway .... you see the turning for Bath. I think it's junction 19, but I'm not absolutely sure.

5. I was so tired I fell asleep .... I got on the train and I missed my stop!

6. My family lived in Italy .... I was 16, so I grew up speaking Italian as well as English.

7. I studied in Germany for a year .... I was 18, so I speak German quite well.

8. Why didn't you visit us .... you came to London? It would've been really nice to see you.

9. I feel really tired. I was studying for my exam .... four o'clock this morning.

10. I didn't go abroad .... I was 19. My parents didn't like travelling or going on planes.

10 Writing – giving directions

Complete the e-mail with the words in the box.

along	cost	see you
come out of	keep going	take

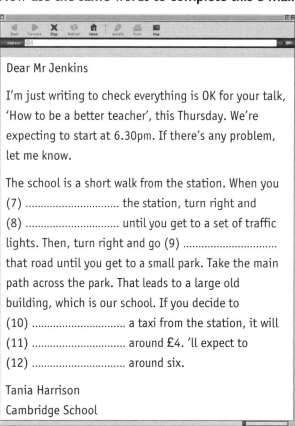

Hi Anoushka,

This is just a quick e-mail to tell you exactly how to get to my house for the dinner tonight.
(1) .... the train to Finsbury Park.
When you (2) .... the station, cross the main road and take the Number 41 bus. Get off at the fourth stop in front of a newsagent's. It will
(3) .... you 70p. When you get off the bus, (4) .... up the road until you get to the end and then turn left. Our house is
.... (5) that road on the left. It's number 68, flat three. (6) .... around 7.30.

Pascal

Now use the same words to complete this e-mail.

Dear Mr Jenkins

I'm just writing to check everything is OK for your talk, 'How to be a better teacher', this Thursday. We're expecting to start at 6.30pm. If there's any problem, let me know.

The school is a short walk from the station. When you
(7) .... the station, turn right and
(8) .... until you get to a set of traffic lights. Then, turn right and go (9) ....
that road until you get to a small park. Take the main path across the park. That leads to a large old building, which is our school. If you decide to
(10) .... a taxi from the station, it will
(11) .... around £4. 'll expect to
(12) .... around six.

Tania Harrison
Cambridge School

Now write a similar e-mail to a friend giving directions to your house.

12 Free time

1 When was the last time?

Match the questions with the answers.

1. When was the last time you went to see a play? ☐
2. When was the last time you went to see a film? ☐
3. When was the last time you went to see a musical? ☐
4. When was the last time you went to see an exhibition? ☐
5. When was the last time you went to a restaurant? ☐
6. When was the last time you went to a concert? ☐
7. When was the last time you did some exercise? ☐
8. When was the last time you went to see a sports match? ☐

a. It was a month or two ago. I saw The Mothers playing in a little club in Hampton. They were great!

b. It was a few weeks ago. I went to see this new Japanese horror movie called *Dark Water*.

c. It was two or three weeks ago. I played volleyball with some friends on the beach.

d. I've never actually been to see one! I can't stand musicals!

e. It was yesterday, actually. I went to this thing at the Photographer's Gallery. It was really good.

f. It was the day before yesterday, actually. We went to a lovely little Greek place near where we live.

g. It was over a year ago. My father took me to see Poland play Estonia.

h. It was about six months ago. *Hamlet* was on at a theatre in town.

2 Conversation

Complete the conversation with ONE word in each space.

E: So what did you (1) .... last night?

F: Oh, I went to (2) .... this new play, *Hello You*, at The Playhouse in town.

E: Oh right. Was it any (3) .... ?

F: Yes, it was OK. I've seen better things.

E: Oh, so do you go to the theatre a (4) .... ?

F: Yes, quite often, maybe (5) .... or twice a month.

E: Wow! That's quite a lot. I (6) .... ever go. I prefer to go to the cinema or just go out with friends.

F: Yes, I've always really liked the theatre. I actually go to a drama club and sing with a group of people as well.

E: Really? So what (7) .... of things do you sing?

F: Lots of things really, but (8) .... musicals – *West Side Story, Chicago*, things like that.

E: That's great. So are you any good? I mean, do you sing solo or what?

F: No. I'm OK, but I'm (9) .... that good. I just like singing.

E: Oh, that's great.

F: What about you? What do you do in your free (10) .... ? Have you got any special hobbies?

Language note: *once or twice*

When we talk about how often we do things, we can say *once a week / month* and *twice a week / month*, but we say *three times a week / month*. We also often say *once or twice a week / month* but *two or three times a week / month*. Notice that it's always the small number which comes first – *three or four times, five or six times*.

3 Adding information

Rewrite the sentences so that all the information is included in one sentence. The first one has been done for you.

1. I went to see a play. The play is called *The Hotel in Amsterdam*. It's on at The Bush Theatre.

   I went to see a / this play, The Hotel in Amsterdam,
   at the Bush Theatre.

2. I stayed in and watched a programme. The programme was called *Holly Oak*. The programme was about Ireland.

   ....

   ....

3. I'm reading a book. The book is called *Upside Down*. The book is about Australia.

   ....

   ....

4. I went to a restaurant. The restaurant is called Lalibella. The restaurant is in Tufnell Park.

   ....

   ....

5. I went to see a new film. The film is called *Down With Love*. I went with my boyfriend.

   ....

   ....

6. I went to see an exhibition. The exhibition was called *The New Modernists*. The exhibition was at the Tate Gallery.

   ....

   ....

4 Do you do that a lot?

Complete the questions with the words in the box.

cook	leave	take	wear
go	see	use	work

1. Do you .... shopping a lot?

2. Do you .... the internet a lot?

3. Do you .... your parents a lot?

4. Do you .... a suit a lot?

5. Do you .... foreign food a lot?

6. Do you .... weekends a lot?

7. Do you .... taxis a lot?

8. Do you .... tips a lot in your country?

Now match the answers with the questions above.

1. ☐ 2. ☐ 3. ☐ 4. ☐

5. ☐ 6. ☐ 7. ☐ 8. ☐

a. Yes, all the time. I read a lot of web diaries and I order things on-line as well. I also download music if it's free.

b. Yes, all the time. It's terrible because I always spend too much on clothes and books!

c. Yes, quite a lot. I try to visit them once every couple of months.

d. Yes, quite a lot – but only if the service is good, of course.

e. No, not that much. I don't really like smart clothes. I prefer to be more casual.

f. No, not that much – but I'm trying to learn how to do some Thai dishes at the moment.

g. No, hardly ever. I usually take the bus, but last night I missed the last one, so I had to get a cab.

h. No, hardly ever. I'm usually completely free. We're just really busy at the office at the moment. My boss asked me to work on Saturday as a favour.

Language note: *free*

Did you notice the two different uses of *free* in the last exercise? We say something is *free* if you don't have to pay for it. Sometimes a museum or exhibition is *free to get into* or is *free for students*. You might get a *free* gift with a magazine or *get free tickets* for a concert.

When we are not busy, we sometimes say we are *free*. We ask *Do you get much free time?* and *Are you free on Saturday night?* You can also tell people to *keep next Sunday free* because you might want to do something together.

5 │ Who do you support?

Match the questions with the answers.

1. Who do you support? ☐
2. How long've you been supporting them? ☐
3. Why do you support them? ☐
4. Who's your favourite player? ☐
5. How're they doing at the moment? ☐
6. Who're their biggest rivals? ☐
7. Do you ever go and see them? ☐

a. Since I was a child.

b. Real Madrid – they're our big enemies!

c. Maybe once or twice a season. I usually just watch them on TV.

d. I've got lots, but Ronaldinho is my favourite at the moment.

e. Barcelona.

f. Oh, my father was a Barcelona fan, so it's part of my family history.

g. Terribly! We didn't win anything last season! Just wait till next season, though!

6 │ Cup or league?

In cup competitions you start with lots of teams and finally finish with two. You can only win or lose. A league is played over several weeks or months. You play lots of games and the team who gets the most points wins. You can win, lose or draw.

Decide if the following people are talking about cup games (C) or league games (L).

1. We're in the quarter finals. ....
2. We're near the bottom of the table. ....
3. We're near the top of the table. ....
4. We won the semi-final on penalties. ....
5. We've drawn the last four matches. ....
6. We lost in the final. ....
7. We got knocked out in the first round. ....
8. We're going to go up this season. ....
9. We're going down to the second division. ....
10. They are a long way ahead. No team is going to catch them. ....
11. There are only three games left of the season. ....
12. They scored in the final minutes of extra time. ....

7 │ Superlatives (1)

Complete the sentences with the superlative form of the adjectives in the box.

fit	lazy	nice	old	tall

1. My friend Rachel is the .... person I know. She goes running every day and swimming three times a week!

2. I'm the .... student in the class. Everyone else is much younger than me.

3. My dad is one of the .... people I know. He never does any exercise – and he never helps my mum with the housework!

4. Wow! Look! He's one of the .... people I've ever seen! He must be over two metres.

5. I met Michael Jordan once. He was great – one of the .... people I've ever met.

Now complete these sentences with the superlative form of the adjectives in the box.

beautiful	interesting	young
easy	relaxed	

6. That was one of the .... exams I've ever taken. I'm sure I've passed!

7. I'm reading *How to talk to your cat* at the moment. It's great. It's one of the .... things I've ever read.

8. I'm one of the .... people in the company. Most people are a lot older than me.

9. She's one of the .... people I know. She never worries about anything.

10. We spent three weeks on an island in the Pacific. It was amazing – one of the .... places I've been to. I loved it!

Language note: *the fittest person*

Did you notice that we use a singular noun when we say *the* + superlative + noun, but when we say *one of the* + superlative + noun, we use a plural noun? For example:
He's the fittest person I know.
It's the best place in town.
He's the best-looking man I've ever seen!
He's one of the fittest people I know.
It's one of the best places in town.
He's one of the best-looking men I've ever seen!

8 Superlatives (2)

Match the sentence beginnings with the sentence endings.

1. It was the poshest hotel ☐
2. That was the most disgusting meal ☐
3. That was one of the best films ☐
4. That's the best computer game ☐
5. It's the best book ☐
6. I think this one here is one of the best photos ☐
7. It's one of the most beautiful countries ☐
8. Miriam's one of the nicest people ☐

a. I've ever had in my life. It was horrible!
b. I've played in a long time. It's brilliant!
c. I've ever taken. I really like it.
d. I know. She's lovely.
e. I've ever stayed in. The view from the room was incredible!
f. I've ever seen. The special effects were amazing!
g. I've read in a long time. It was really good.
h. I've ever been to. The scenery was incredible!

9 Photos

Complete the conversation with the words in the box.

cheese	further	smile	taking
closer	light	take	the zoom
fit	press		

A: Excuse me. Would you mind (1) .... a photo for us?

B: Of course not. Which button should I (2) .... ?

A: This one here, and press this one if you want to adjust (3) ....

B: OK, fine. Can you stand a bit (4) .... together or move (5) .... back? I can't (6) .... you all into the picture. OK, that's it. Ready everyone and (7) .... That's great.

A: Could you just (8) .... another one. Just in case.

B: Yes, sure. Do you think we need the flash?

A: I don't think so. There's quite a lot of (9) ....

B: OK everyone. Say 'cheese'.

A: (10) .... !

B: Thanks very much.

A: No problem.

10 Present simple for talking about the future

Complete the story with the present simple form of the verbs in the box.

be	kick off	leave
finish	last	start
get into		

This weekend is going to be very busy for me. I'm going to Cologne to stay with a friend. My flight (1) .... London at seven o'clock on Friday night and (2) .... Cologne at 10.30. I (3) .... work at 4.30, so I'll have to take a taxi to the airport. That'll be expensive. I (4) .... work at six in the morning, so I'll be really tired by the time I get to Germany. Saturday (5) .... my friend's birthday, so I'm going to take him to see a football match. I think it (6) .... at three o'clock and (7) .... for an hour and a half. I'm really looking forward to it.

11 Know how to

Complete the sentences with *how to* and the verbs in the box.

boil	drive	play	set up
develop	get	serve	ski

1. The photography course I'm doing is great. I'm learning .... my own pictures.
2. I'd like to take driving lessons sometime soon. It's embarrassing. I'm 35 and I don't know ....
3. My wife wants to go to Switzerland this winter, but I'm too scared to learn .... !
4. Wow! You're really good at tennis. Could you teach me .... as well as you?
5. I'd like to do a computing course and learn .... websites.
6. He's absolutely useless at cooking. He doesn't even know .... an egg!
7. I took piano classes for ages, but I never really learned .... anything. I was useless!
8. I don't know .... to your house. Could you draw me a map?

1 Using vocabulary: places to stay

Match the beginnings of the conversations with A's follow-up comments.

1. A: We stayed in this horrible campsite near the town.
   B: Oh dear. What was wrong with it? ☐

2. A: We stayed in this horrible hotel in the centre of town.
   B: Oh dear. What was wrong with it? ☐

3. A: We stayed in this awful little bed and breakfast on the seafront.
   B: Oh dear. What was wrong with it? ☐

4. A: We rented this villa in the mountains, but it was awful.
   B: Oh dear. What was wrong with it? ☐

5. A: We were going to stay with some friends for a week, but we went to a hotel after a couple of days.
   B: Oh right, why was that? ☐

6. A: We were going to travel round the country, but we ended up staying in one place.
   B: Oh right, why was that? ☐

a. There was no electricity or hot water! The kitchen had a little gas stove, but there was no other heating.

b. The place was almost empty, but they gave us a damp room looking over a building site instead of the beach.

c. It was really crowded. We hardly had enough space to pitch the tent.

d. James twisted his ankle on the second day we were there, so he couldn't carry his backpack.

e. They've got a baby and he just screamed all night. We just couldn't sleep.

f. The rooms were tiny and it was right next to a bar, so it was very noisy at night.

Complete each expression from the conversations with ONE word.

g. to .... the tent

h. There was no .... or hot water!

i. a gas ....

j. a damp ....

k. a building ....

l. .... his ankle

m. the baby .... all night

2 Booking a room in a hotel

Complete the end of the conversation with ONE word in each space.

R: That'll be £475. We'll need to (1) .... your credit card details to make the (2) ....

A: Yes, sure.

R: What kind of card are you (3) .... with?

A: Visa.

R: OK. And the (4) .... ?

A: 5362 3870 6429 8479.

R: That's fine. And what's the (5) .... date?

A: 06 / 09.

R: OK. And your name as it appears (6) .... the card?

A: Yurick. That's Y-U-R-I-C-K.

R: Great. So that's all (7) .... for you, sir. We'll look (8) .... to seeing you on the 19th.

A: Yes, actually, there is one more thing. I need (9) .... of the booking for my visa application.

R: Of course, no problem sir. If you fax us (10) .... your request, we'll fax you back a letter by tomorrow.

A: Great. If you (11) .... a second, I'll get a pen. Yes, what's the fax number?

R: 0044 31 569 4482.

A: OK, that's great. You've (12) .... very helpful. Thanks.

R: No problem.

3 First conditionals

Complete the sentences with the present simple or *will* form of the verbs.

1. I .... you a hand if you ....
   (give, want)

2. I .... and get some if you ....
   (go, like)

3. I .... you there if you ....
   (take, like)

4. I .... a copy of the photo for you if you
   .... (make, like)

5. I .... it later if I .... time.
   (do, have)

6. I .... with you if I .... , but
   I'd rather not. (come, have to)

7. I .... you if you can't ....
   anyone else, but I'd rather not. (help, find)

8. The tickets .... more expensive if
   we .... them now. (be, not buy)

9. The situation .... just .... if
   we .... anything now. (get worse, not do)

10. The show .... if we .... the
    tickets now. (sell out, not get)

4 Hardly

Complete the sentences with the words in the box.

hardly any	hardly breathe	hardly ever
hardly anyone	hardly done	hardly hear
hardly anything	hardly eaten	

1. A: I love going to the cinema. I go all the time.
   B: Really? I .... go. I prefer
      to wait for films to come out on video.

2. A: Do you want something to eat?
   B: Yes, I'm starving. I've
      .... anything all day.

3. A: What was the place you stayed in like?
   B: It was nice. There was ....
      staying there, so we got extra-special treatment.

4. It was really horrible. There were so many people
   crowded on the train I could ....

5. A: What did you do over the weekend?
   B: .... I just sat round
      the house and took it easy.

6. A: There's .... coffee left.
      Shall I make a fresh pot?
   B: Not for me. I've had enough, thanks.

7. A: Have you had a good day?
   B: Not really. I've .... any
      of the things I wanted to do.

8. Honestly, the noise was so loud I could
   .... myself speak, and I
   couldn't hear the students at all.

5 Almost everyone / hardly anyone

Complete the sentences with the words in the box.

all	all	always	any	any	every	no

1. I work late almost .... night of the week.

2. I've seen almost .... his films.

3. I hardly have .... money. I'm broke.

4. Almost .... the best places to visit are in
   the south of the country.

5. There are hardly .... places worth
   visiting in that town.

6. There's almost .... inflation in my country
   at the moment. Prices have hardly gone up at all.

7. We almost .... go to Spain for our
   holidays.

6 Key word: *stay*

Find twelve expressions with the word stay. Mark the end of each expression using /.

stayeduplatestayinalldaystayscoolstayedin
bedallmorningstayfordinnerhowlongare
youstayingstaytilltheendwhereareyou
stayingstaythenightitwon'tstayonwhattim
edoesthatbarstayopentilleverythingjust
staysthesame

Test yourself. Spend five minutes memorising the expressions with *stay*. Then cover the expressions and complete the sentences. How many expressions did you get right?

1. I just .... because I needed to catch up on my sleep.

2. I couldn't .... of the meeting because I had to go somewhere else.

3. I .... last night to finish some work.

4. The weather was so bad on Saturday we had to ....

5. You've missed the last bus. Do you want to .... here? We've got a spare room.

6. He's very calm. He always .... under pressure.

7. I've tried sticking it with sellotape, but ....

8. We have a lot of meetings about changing things, but then ....

9. A: OK. I'm going to go and leave you to eat in peace.
   B: Are you sure you don't want to .... ? There's plenty for everyone.

10. A: .... ?
    B: In a small guest house on the outskirts of town.

11. A: .... ?
    B: I don't think it ever closes, does it?

12. A: .... ?
    B: Until I get fed up with being here.

7 As long as

Match the questions with the answers.

1. Is it OK if I meet you in the pub a bit later? ☐
2. Do you mind if I watch a documentary on Channel 4 later? ☐
3. Is it OK if I use the telephone? ☐
4. Is it OK if I have a beer from the fridge? ☐
5. Do you mind if I have a shower? ☐
6. Do you mind if we have a small party here on Sunday? ☐
7. Do you mind if I make myself something to eat? ☐
8. Is it OK if I just check out something on the internet? ☐

a. Of course not, as long as it's not on at the same time as the golf. It's the final round of the Masters.

b. Of course, as long as you're not phoning New Zealand!

c. Yes, go ahead, as long as it's not a site you shouldn't be looking at!

d. Of course not, as long as you clear up after yourself when you've finished cooking.

e. Yes, as long as it's not the last one!

f. Of course, as long as you're there by nine. We'll probably go somewhere else after that.

g. As long as you're quick. We're already a bit late leaving.

h. Not really, as long as you don't make too much mess and it doesn't go on too late.

Language note: *check out*

If you *check out something* or *check something out*, you have a look at it to see if you think it's good. When we want to recommend things, we often tell friends they *should check out this website*, *check this new bookshop out* or *check out the new club in town*.

8 Key words for writing: *because of* and *despite*

Because and ***because of*** **have a very similar meaning. For example:**

- Our plane was cancelled *because there was a strike* at the airport.
- Our plane was cancelled *because of a strike* at the airport.

Even though **and** ***despite*** **have a very similar meaning. For example:**

- We had a really nice time, *even though the weather was awful.*
- We had a really nice time *despite the awful weather.*

In each case the difference between the two sentences is in the grammar that follows the linking word.

Because **and** ***even though*** **begin a verb clause.**

- *Because the hotel was very quiet,* they gave us two double rooms for the price of two singles.
- The hotel still got it wrong e*ven though I e-mailed to confirm our booking.*

Because of **and** ***despite*** **are followed by a noun or an** *-ing* **form.**

- My husband was late, so I was late *because of* him.
- *Despite writing down* all the directions, I got lost.

Complete the sentences with *despite* or *because of.*

1. We were late .... the heavy traffic.

2. We got there on time .... the heavy traffic.

3. There was a really bad traffic jam .... a car crash which blocked the road.

4. We had a lovely time .... the fact it rained all week.

5. He forgot to buy any film for the camera .... the fact I told him to do it about five times.

6. The plane was delayed for six hours .... a strike by air-traffic controllers.

7. I got sunburnt .... putting on factor 25 sun cream.

8. We had a terrible time, just .... her complaining about everything all the time. It was so boring!

9 Writing

Choose the correct words to complete this letter.

Dear Bryan,

I've just (1) .... back from holiday and despite the terrible journey there, we (2) .... a great time. First of all, our flight was (3) .... for four hours because of a problem with the plane. When we (4) .... in London, it was raining, but we didn't have (5) .... umbrella or a raincoat. We didn't have any English money and the bank was closed, (6) .... we had to walk to the hotel. When we got there, we were very wet. (7) .... we booked the room weeks before we left the States, the hotel didn't have any (8) .... of our booking. They had a huge suite, (9) .... , which normally cost £500 a night. However, because they had made the mistake, and because we were quite angry, they gave us the room for £100 per night! After that, we were much happier, and we lived like kings (10) .... we came back home! It's a shame I have to go back to work!

We must go out for a drink sometime and I'll tell you more about it. Give me a ring.

Hank

1. A returned	B got	C gone	D went
2. A spent	B made	C did	D had
3. A delayed	B cancelled	C waited	D stopped
4. A arrived	B got	C went	D came
5. A the	B any	C an	D some
6. A but	B so	C then	D because
7. A Despite	B However	C Because	D Even though
8. A writing	B record	C proofs	D receipt
9. A though	B although	C but	D so
10. and then	B when	C until	D A because of

Now write your own e-mail, telling a friend about a terrible journey or holiday.

14 What was it like?

1 Good times, bad times

What was your holiday like? Match the beginnings and endings of the answers to this question.

1. We missed ☐
2. My husband's company paid ☐
3. I made lots of ☐
4. The flight was delayed ☐
5. The airline company lost ☐
6. Everyone treated ☐

a. us really well.
b. for six hours.
c. my bags on the flight out to New Zealand.
d. new friends.
e. our flight.
f. for everything while we were there.

Now match these beginnings and endings of the answers.

7. I had my bag ☐
8. It rained ☐
9. The weather ☐
10. I met lots of ☐
11. We had ☐
12. There was a problem ☐

g. old friends again.
h. with my visa and they wouldn't let me into the country.
i. the whole time we were there.
j. was amazing the whole time we were there.
k. the whole beach to ourselves.
l. stolen while we were there.

Decide which sentences have these meanings.

We had a great time. ☐ ☐ ☐ ☐ ☐

We had a terrible time. ☐ ☐ ☐ ☐ ☐

Language note: *treat*

It's important to *treat people with respect* – to talk to them and behave towards them with respect. Some bosses *treat their workers really badly* and some husbands *treat their wives like dirt*. Have you ever had a teacher who *treated you like a child* or *treated some students better than others*?

2 Conversation

Complete the conversation with ONE word in each space.

M: Hello, Tom. Are you all right? I haven't seen you (1) .... a while.

T: Yes, I'm fine. I was in the States all last week visiting a friend of (2) .... I thought I'd told you about it.

M: No, I don't (3) .... so. So whereabouts did you go?

T: (4) .... of the time I was in Boston where my friend lives, but I went up to New York for a (5) .... of days.

M: Right. So what was it (6) .... ?

T: It was great. New York was amazing. It's just (7) .... a lively place, there's a real mixture of people, and the food's great.

M: Yes? What (8) .... Boston? What was that like?

T: Oh, it's nice. It's quite an interesting place. I didn't do (9) .... there – mainly just (10) .... time with my friend – but it was good. I met a lot of his friends and they were really nice and friendly.

M: Sounds great. I'm quite jealous.

T: Have you (11) .... been to the States?

M: Yes, I (12) .... there about three years ago, but I went to the West Coast.

Write a conversation between YOU and a friend about a holiday you've been on. For example:

F: Are you all right? I haven't seen you for a while.

Y: Yes, I'm fine. I was in Spain last week ...

3 Talking about your experiences

Put the sentences in order and make a conversation.

Conversation 1

a. I don't know, I haven't actually been there, but I'm thinking of taking Geri there for her birthday.

b. Yes, that's what I thought.

c. Have you ever been to that restaurant on Grove Road?

d. I don't know. It looks nice from the outside.

e. No, what's it like?

1. ☐ 2. ☐ 3. ☐ 4. ☐

Now complete these conversations with the words in the boxes.

Conversation 2

| actually | day | nice | tasted | think | time |

A: I had snake for the first (1) .... the other (2) .... Have you ever had it?

B: Yes, I have (3) .... I had some when I was on holiday in Hong Kong.

A: Oh right, what did you (4) .... of it?

B: It was all right. It just (5) .... a bit like chicken to me.

A: Really? I must say, I didn't think it was very (6) ....

Conversation 3

doing	for	studying	travel
ever	going	there	whereabouts
first	speak		

A: Have you (1) .... been to China?

B: Yes, I lived in Beijing (2) .... a year.

A: Really? What were you (3) .... there? Were you working there?

B: No, I was (4) .... Chinese.

A: Really? So do you (5) .... Chinese well?

B: Yes, quite well.

A: Wow, that's brilliant. I'm (6) .... to go there this summer.

B: Oh yes. Have you been (7) .... before?

A: No, it'll be my (8) .... time.

B: You'll love it. (9) .... are you going?

A: I'm flying to Hong Kong and then I'm going to (10) .... round the mainland.

4 Answering *Have you ever ... ?* questions

Put the words in brackets in order and complete the answers to the question above.

1. No, never, ...
(love / I'd / but / to)

2. No, never, ...
(always / but / to / wanted / I've)

3. No, never, ...
(to / be / supposed / but / brilliant / it's)

4. No, never, ...
(to / really / but / never / I've / wanted)

5. Yes, I have actually, ...
(it / I / like / but / really / didn't)

6. Yes, I have actually, ...
(I'd / sure / but / not / again / it / I'm / do)

7. Yes, I have, actually – ....
(times / quite / a / few)

8. Yes, I have actually. ....
(couple / years / now / a / was / ago / it / of)

5 He's always complaining!

Match each sentence with two follow-up sentences.

1. My dad is always complaining about the government. ☐ ☐
2. My dad is always complaining about the weather. ☐ ☐
3. My dad is always complaining about work. ☐ ☐
4. My dad is always complaining about banks. ☐ ☐
5. My mum is always complaining about my dad. ☐ ☐

a. He says it's impossible for him to get a loan from them.

b. She says he never stops complaining!

c. He says he's not paid enough for the work he does.

d. He says it's too humid at this time of year.

e. He says his boss is a terrible bully.

f. She says he should help with the housework more.

g. He says they keep putting taxes up.

h. He says it pours with rain all the time.

i. He says they should do something about unemployment.

j. He says they charge too much interest.

6 Expressions with *have*

Put the words in order and make sentences.

a. had / I / virus / this / horrible

....

b. we / a / had / time / great

....

c. an / I / argument / had

....

d. do / something / to / to / you / want / go / and / have / eat?

....

e. terrible / had / I / a / time

....

f. have / had / you / anything / to / eat?

....

g. I / had / appointment / an

....

h. haven't / had / to / I / eat / anything

....

i. to / off / have / I / week / had / the / whole

....

j. big / I / a / had / breakfast

....

Now translate the expressions above into your language.

a. ....

b. ....

c. ....

d. ....

e. ....

f. ....

g. ....

h. ....

i. ....

j. ....

Complete the conversations with the expressions with *have*.

1. A: How was your holiday?
   B: Oh, ... The place was fantastic and it was really sunny the whole time we were there. It was great.

2. A What was that party like last night?
   B: It was awful. .... I wish I'd stayed at home.

3. A: .... I'm going to make some pasta, if you'd like some.
   B: Yes, that'd be great. I'm starving. .... all day.

4. A: Are you all right? I didn't see you last week.
   B: I know, ... I had a temperature, I felt sick, I had a really bad headache. It was awful. .... from work.

5. A: .... ?
   B: Yes, I'm quite hungry. Where do you want to go?

6. A: Are you hungry?
   B: No, I'm fine actually. .... this morning.

7. A: Are you OK? You look a bit upset.
   B: Yes, I'll be OK in a moment. .... with some guy in a car on the way here. He was so stupid! He was just really horrible to me.

8. A: I'm sorry I wasn't at the class on Tuesday. .... at the dentist.
   B: Don't worry. Maybe you could ask Yumiko to show you what we did.

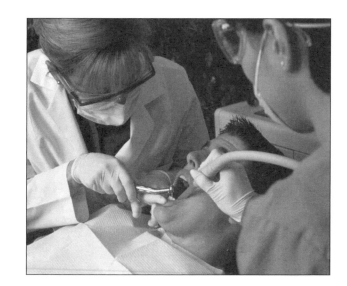

7 | Asking what things are like

Match the questions with the second parts of the answers.

1. A: What's your sister like?
   B: She's OK, I suppose. ☐

2. A: What's your new flat like?
   B: It's OK, I suppose. ☐

3. A: What was the concert like?
   B: Great! ☐

4. A: What was your holiday in England like?
   B: Awful! ☐

5. A: What's the area you live in like?
   B: It's great. ☐

6. A: What's the course you're doing like?
   B: Not very good, actually. ☐

7. A: What was that film you saw the
      other day like?
   B: Brilliant. ☐

a. It's nice and green – it's near a park and there are lots of trees in my road.

b. We had a really bad time. The weather was awful, the people were very unfriendly. Honestly, it was terrible!

c. We're not very close. We don't get on very well and we don't see each other very much either.

d. It was one of the best performances of that piece I've ever heard.

e. It's quite cramped now we've moved all our stuff in. It's quite old too, so it's a bit cold at night.

f. It was great – the acting, the story, everything! You should go and see it.

g. The teacher just talks and talks and talks, and we just have to sit there and listen. It's really boring!

Complete each expression from the conversations with ONE word.

i. We're not .... close.

j. We don't .... on very well.

k. We don't see each other very .... either.

l. Our new flat is quite ....

8 | Asking longer questions

Make longer questions using the ideas given. The first one has been done for you.

1. I know you saw a film yesterday. I want to know about it.
   I ask: *What was that film you saw yesterday like?*

2. I know you stayed in a hotel in Naples. I want to know about it.
   I ask: What was that .... like?

3. I know you play tennis with a guy. I want to know about him.
   I ask: What's that .... like?

4. I know your brother works for a company. I want to know about it.
   I ask: What's that .... like?

5. I know you've moved. I want to know about the area.
   I ask: ....

6. I know you went to a party at Colin's house. I want to know about it.
   I ask: ....

7. I know you went to see a play last week. I want to know about it.
   I ask: ....

8. I know you and your boyfriend went to a Chinese restaurant last week. I want to know about it.
   I ask: ....

Remember that when we're talking to someone who knows <u>which</u> thing we're talking about – or if we make it clear which thing we mean – we say *that* thing.

Language note: *cramped*

If a place is *crowded*, there are too many people. Pubs, shops and trains can be *really crowded*.

If a room is *cramped*, it's too small and there's too much furniture in it. In a small classroom, maybe you feel a bit *cramped for space*. Is it *a bit cramped* in your bedroom or have you got *plenty of space*?

15 What's on?

1 Films

Match the sentences with the follow-up sentences.

1. It's a French film. ☐
2. It's a comedy. ☐
3. It's a love story. ☐
4. It's a martial arts film. ☐
5. It's an action movie. ☐
6. It's a horror film. ☐

a. The fight scenes are really good.
b. The special effects are fantastic.
c. It's really funny.
d. It's really scary.
e. It's really moving.
f. It's got subtitles in English.

2 Conversation

Complete the conversation with ONE word in each space.

I: What are you doing tonight?

J: I've got nothing (1) .... What about you?

I: Well, I was thinking of going to the cinema. Do you want to come with me?

J: Yes, maybe. What are you thinking of (2) .... ?

I: Have you seen *Lands of Hope* yet? It's (3) .... to be really good.

J: Yes, I saw it (4) .... week. It's OK, but it's not brilliant. What (5) .... is on?

I: Well, there's a film with George Clooney.

J: Oh, yes? I don't (6) .... like him.

I: No, neither (7) .... I. And then there's this film, *City of Dreams*.

J: I haven't heard of it. What's it (8) .... ?

I: It's a French film. It's a drama about some Algerians growing up in Paris. It's got quite a good (9) ....

J: It sounds quite interesting. What time's it (10) .... ?

I: 6.30, 8.15 and 11.20.

J: And (11) .... 's it on?

I: The ABC.

J: OK. Well, (12) .... we go to the 8.15 showing? I want to have (13) .... to eat before we go.

I: Yes, OK. Shall I meet you (14) .... , then? You know where it is, don't you?

J: Yes. So I (15) .... see you there around eight. If I'm there first, shall I get the tickets?

I: Yes. Fine.

Can you remember where the pauses and the stressed sounds are in this conversation? Mark the pauses // and underline the stressed syllables. For example:

A: What are you <u>do</u>ing to<u>night</u>?
B: I've got <u>nothing</u> <u>planned</u>. // What about <u>you</u>?

Compare your ideas about the pauses and stressed sounds with the tapescript in the Coursebook.

3 Questions about films and programmes

Complete the conversations with the questions in the box. Use each question twice.

What time's it on?	Where's it on?
What's it about?	Who's in it?
What's on?	Who's it by?

1. A: ....
    B: I haven't heard her name before. I think it's the first film she's directed.

2. A: ....
    B: Robin Williams, Jennifer Lopez and Jackie Chan.

3. A: ....
    B: I'm not sure, but I'm sure they'll be showing it at the Cineworld.

4. A: ....
    B: *Terminator 5*.

5. A: ....
    B: 7.30 and 10.20.

6. A: ....
    B: Steven Spielberg.

7. A: ....
    B: I don't know. I need to phone to check. What's the earliest you can go?

8. A: ....
    B: It's an action movie about these people trying to take over the world.

9. A: ....
    B: I don't know that much about it, to be honest. I think it's a science fiction film.

10. A: ....
    B: The Odeon.

11. A: ....
    B: Nothing much. There's been nothing good on for ages.

12. A: ....
    B: Tom Conti and some other people I've never heard of.

Write a conversation between YOU and a friend like that in Exercise 2. Arrange to go to the cinema. Talk about a real film you'd like to see at the moment. For example:

F: I was thinking of going to the cinema this evening. Do you want to come?
Y: What are you thinking of going to see?

4 Famous people

Complete the sentences with the words in the box.

developed	made	presents
invented	paints	writes
leads	plays	

1. He's a famous TV personality. He .... a sports programme.

2. He's a famous film star. He usually .... action heroes.

3. She's a famous singer. She's .... hundreds of records.

4. He's a famous artist. He mainly .... portraits.

5. He's an author. He mainly .... novels.

6. He's a famous inventor. He .... the light bulb.

7. He's a politician. He .... the main opposition party in my country. He's quite right wing.

8. He's a famous scientist. He .... the theory of relativity.

5 Meeting a famous person

Choose the correct words to complete the story.

I (1) .... met the president of my country in Belgium. I (2) .... there at the time and I (3) .... to this big party at the Embassy to (4) .... our Independence Day. Anyway, the president was there. I even (5) .... his hand and had my photo (6) .... with him. It was funny, because he looked quite different in (7) .... life. He was (8) .... shorter than I expected.

1.	A once	B often	C was	D have
2.	A lived	B have stayed	C was living	D stayed
3.	A invited	B invitation	C was invited	D invite
4.	A celebrate	B celebration	C remember	D remind
5.	A extended	B shook	C was holding	D took
6.	A took	B taken	C make	D made
7.	A real	B human	C actual	D daily
8.	A very	B more	C quite	D a lot

6 TV and video

Complete the conversations with the words in the box.

record	turn the TV down
rewind	turn the TV on
set the video	turn the TV up
turn over	turned it off

1. A: Can you .... ? I can
      hardly hear it.
   B: You must be going deaf! It's quite loud.

2. A: Can you .... to
      Channel 5? There's a film I want to watch which
      is starting in a minute.
   B: Can't you .... it? I'm in
      the middle of watching this programme.

3. A: I'm going to miss the last part of that series,
      Hanging On, when we're out. Can you
      .... to record it? It's on
      BBC3.
   B: Yes, of course, what time does it start?

4. A: What did she say?
   B: I'm not sure. Why don't you stop the video and
      .... it a bit?

5. A: Could you .... a bit? It's
      a bit loud.
   B: Why don't you do it? You've got the remote
      control!

6. A: Do you mind if I ....
      and see if there's anything worth watching?
   A: I've already checked and there isn't anything on.
      That's why I .... !

Language note: *drama*

A *drama* is a play written for TV, the theatre or the
radio. There are *TV dramas* and *radio dramas*. If the
drama is set in the past and all the actors are wearing
clothes from that time, it's a *costume drama*. On TV,
you often get *police dramas*, *family dramas*, *historical
dramas* and *hospital dramas*.

7 What does it say in the TV guide?

Does the reviewer of these films think they are
good or bad? Underline the words which tell you
the reviewer's opinion.

1. Dull romance between a cleaner
   and her boss. ....

2. Genuinely scary horror film that
   will have you jumping out
   of your seat. ....

3. Fascinating documentary about
   life in Nepal. ....

4. Brilliant drama based on the
   novel by Jack Higgins. ....

5. Moving drama of life in the
   concentration camps. ....

6. Dreadful comedy starring
   Hugh Grant. ....

7. Very over-rated Oscar winner. ....

8. Enjoyable romantic comedy
   starring Meg Ryan. ....

8 The passive or active?

Choose the correct form.

1. Sorry, I'm so late. My train *delayed / was delayed* by
   about an hour.
2. We didn't go to the show in the end, because it
   cancelled / was cancelled.
3. I had to *cancel / be cancelled* my credit card because
   it *stole / was stolen*.
4. Do you want to *pick up / be picked up* from the
   airport?
5. Did you see what *happened / was happened* in Paris
   yesterday?
6. It was a bit embarrassing. I *caught / was caught*
   without a ticket on the bus.
7. We only just *caught / was caught* the train. I think
   we got there a minute before it left.
8. I *woke up / got woken up* by this horrible dog barking
   outside my window.
9. It *stars / is starred* John Wayne.
10. It *directed / was directed* by Sofia Coppola.

Language note: *star and crash*

The verb *star* is never in the passive. We *say the film
stars Nicole Kidman* or *Nicole Kidman stars in the film*.
The verb *crash* is the same. You *say I crashed my
parents' car* or *The car crashed into a wall*. Look out for
other verbs like this.

9 | Key words for writing: *if, what, how, where* and *when*

We use 'question' words after some verbs and in some typical expressions in writing. Note that the word order is **NOT** like a question. For example:

• Just a quick e-mail to see *when you're coming to visit.* (NOT <s>when are you coming</s> …)

Complete the sentences with the words in the box.

how	if	if	if	what	what time

1. Just a quick e-mail to see .... you are.

2. Just a quick e-mail to see .... you got back safely last night.

3. Just a quick e-mail to check .... the class starts tomorrow morning.

4. I am writing to find out .... courses your centre runs.

5. I am writing to find out .... you have any vacancies on the photography course starting next week.

6. I was wondering .... you could help me.

Now complete these sentences with the words in the box.

how long	how much	when
how many	if	which

7. Your brochure doesn't mention .... the intensive course costs.

8. Your website doesn't say .... people are in each class.

9. The advertisement doesn't mention .... the course lasts.

10. The advertisement doesn't say .... dates you are running the courses.

11. I would be grateful .... you could let me know as soon as possible.

12. E-mail me back .... you get this.

10 | Writing letters of enquiry

Complete the letter with the words in the box.

clarify	look forward to
doesn't say	to your website
find out	wanted to know
further information	worried

Dear Sir / Madam

I am writing to ask for (1) .... about the German courses you offer at your school.

According (2) .... , you have six different classes, but it (3) .... exactly what level each class is, and I (4) .... if you take absolute beginners. I am (5) .... that I may be at too low a level for your classes. I also wanted to (6) .... the actual prices for each course. The website says that fees start at £500 for a 14–week course, but it doesn't mention what the maximum price is or if you run intensive courses. I would be most grateful if you could (7) .... this.

I thank you in advance for your assistance and I (8) .... hearing from you soon.

Yours faithfully

Ashley Cole

Now write your own letter of request, asking for information about a course you would like to do. Try to use as many of the expressions below as you can.

Dear Sir / Madam

I am writing to ask for further information about …

According to your brochure / your website / your advertisement, … but it doesn't mention / it doesn't say exactly … so I would be (most) grateful if you could clarify that for me.

I also wanted to know …

I thank you in advance for your assistance and I look forward to hearing from you soon.

Yours faithfully

16 Telephoning

1 Key word: *phone*

Match the sentence beginnings with the endings.

1. I just need to make ☐
2. My flatmates spend ☐
3. Have you tried looking ☐
4. I was so angry I put ☐
5. I don't feel very well. I think I'll phone ☐

a. hours on the phone every evening!
b. the phone down on her.
c. in sick today.
d. a quick phone call.
e. his number up in the phone book?

Now match these sentence beginnings with the endings.

6. Her number's not listed ☐
7. Can I get a £5 phone ☐
8. Maybe we should book ☐
9. I'm in the bath. Answer ☐
10. If I have time, I'll give you ☐

f. card, please?
g. the phone somebody – please!
h. a ring tomorrow, OK?
i. in the phone book.
j. over the phone.

Complete each expression from the sentences with ONE word.

k. make a quick phone ....
l. spend hours .... the phone
m. put the phone down .... her
n. phone .... sick
o. in the phone ....

Language note: *listed*

When a number is not listed in the telephone directory, we often say it is *ex-directory*. *List* is more common as a noun. We *make a shopping list* or *write a guest list* for a party. We say *you forgot to write something on your list* and *your name is not on the list*. When you have *a list of things* which you need to do, the most important things are *at the top of your list* and the least important are *low on your list of priorities*.

2 Conversation

Complete the conversation with ONE word in each space.

J: Hello.

P: Hi, is Jenny (1) .... ?

J: Speaking.

P: Oh right, hi. My (2) ....'s Paola. I'm a friend of Fernanda. We go to the (3) .... school to learn English.

J: Oh, OK. She (4) .... me about you. How are you?

P: Fine, thanks.

J: And how's Fernanda?

P: Oh great. She told me to (5) .... hello. Anyway, I was wondering if you could (6) .... me.

J: I'll try.

P: I'm coming to London for a (7) .... days for a visit and Fernanda said you might be (8) .... to recommend somewhere cheap to stay.

J: Well, you could stay with me if you like. I've got a (9) .... room.

P: Really? Are you sure?

J: Yes, it's no trouble. When are you coming?

P: In two weeks' (10) .... I'm coming down on the Friday and then I'm going to go back on the Tuesday.

J: Fine. Do you want to (11) .... me a ring a bit nearer the time just to check what time you'll be here?

P: Yes, OK.

J: OK, well, I'll speak to you then. Can you say hi to Fernanda from me and (12) .... her for the birthday card? I'll give her a ring next week sometime. I'm actually going away for a few days.

P: OK. Great.

J: See you.

P Yes, bye. And thanks for the offer. It's really kind of you.

J: No problem. Bye.

3 Answering the phone

Complete the sentences with 'll, might or 's.

1. Sorry, she's not here at the moment. She .... probably be back around four.

2. He's away on business at the moment, I'm afraid, but he .... be back tomorrow morning, unless his flight is cancelled or something. Shall I get him to ring you when he gets in?

3. I'm afraid she's gone out for lunch. She .... normally back in the office by one, so try sometime after that.

4. She's away for a week, but she .... phone – she sometimes does when she's out of the office. Do you want to leave a message?

5. He's off sick. I suppose he .... be back at work tomorrow, but he did sound really ill when I spoke to him. He .... be off for several days. Can I help you at all?

6. I'm not sure, actually. He .... not usually around at this time, but I suppose he .... be in the building somewhere. I'll just go and ask if anyone's seen him.

Language note: get him to ring you

I'll get him to ring you means 'I'll ask him to ring you.' You can *get your dad to have a look at your car, get someone to fix your TV* and *get someone to do something for you.*

4 Prepositions

Complete the sentences with the words in the box. Use some words twice.

at	between	in	off	on	out

1. I'm afraid he's not .... the office at the moment.

2. I'm afraid she's away .... holiday until next week.

3. I'm afraid he's .... of the office at the moment.

4. I'm afraid it's her day .... today.

5. I'm afraid he's .... the bathroom at the moment.

6. I'm afraid she's just gone .... for lunch.

7. I'm afraid he's .... sick today.

8. She should be back sometime .... nine and ten tomorrow morning.

9. He'll be back .... the 24th.

10. She said she'll be back .... two.

5 Summarising expressions

Complete the summarising expressions with the words in the box.

annoying	funny
embarrassing	horrible

1. It was really .... ! My face went bright red!

2. It was really .... ! I was really angry about it.

3. It was really .... ! I laughed until I cried!

4. It was really .... ! I felt awful afterwards.

Match the situations with the sentences above.

1. ☐   2. ☐   3. ☐   4. ☐

a. The post office lost the letter you sent me. They said there's nothing they can do about it.

b. I had a hole in my trousers and everyone could see my underwear.

c. I hit a dog while I was driving and it was hurt really badly.

d. The boss burped in the middle of his speech.

Now complete these summarising expressions with the words in the box.

amazing	disgusting
depressing	frightening

5. It was really .... I thought I was going to die.

6. It was .... ! I had a really brilliant time.

7. It was really .... I was really upset about it afterwards.

8. It was .... ! I thought I was going to be sick!

Now match these situations with the sentences above.

5. ☐   6. ☐   7. ☐   8. ☐

e. I went to Buenos Aires on holiday for a week.

f. The storm was so bad the plane had to land in a field.

g. She'd cooked chicken, but with a spicy chocolate sauce!

h. I was there when my great-grandfather died when I was a teenager.

6 -ed / -ing adjectives

Complete the sentences with the words in the box.

annoyed	excited	interested
annoying	exciting	interesting
bored	frightened	
boring	frightening	

1. I'm not very .... in politics. Are you?

2. It was the most .... thing that's ever happened to me. I really thought I was going to die!

3. They tried to overcharge us in the restaurant. I was really .... about it.

4. My son still has lots of bad dreams. He's probably .... of the dark.

5. I was so .... with that film I fell asleep in the middle of it.

6. I couldn't sleep last night because I was so .... about my trip to Japan!

7. It was so .... I fell asleep in the middle of it.

8. It was a really .... game. England scored the winner in the last minute!

9. The cash machine ate my cash card. It was really .... !

10. She's one of the most .... people I've ever met. She's been to 106 different countries!

Language note: frightened of the dark

If you're *frightened of the dark*, you're *scared of it, afraid of it*. All three expressions mean the same thing. Some people are *afraid of snakes*, others are *scared of flying* and some are *frightened to go out of the house at night*. If you're in a frightening situation, you can say *I'm frightened* or *I'm scared*. We don't usually say *I'm afraid* on its own.

7 Texting

Write the abbreviations next to the meanings.

afda	ala	atm	b4n	ltns	oic	wan2	xlnt

1. as long as ....

2. Oh, I see ....

3. excellent ....

4. Long time, no see ....

5. at the moment ....

6. a few days ago ....

7. want to ....

8. Bye for now ....

Can you remember how you write these messages from the Coursebook when you're texting?

9. Great news! ....

10. See you later. ....

11. It's easy. ....

12. Thanks for the information. ....

13. Are you OK? ....

14. Mind your own business! ....

15. See you tonight. ....

16. It's up to you. ....

17. See you tomorrow. ....

18. Can you do it as soon as possible? ....

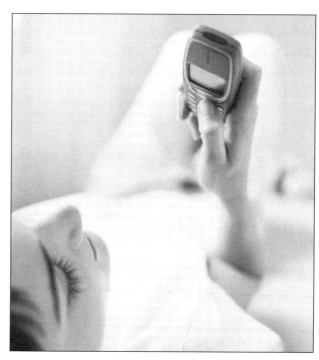

8 Reporting speech (1)

Match the sentence beginnings with the endings.

1. Melanie told me to ask you if ☐
2. Jill told me to say ☐
3. Ron told me to tell you ☐
4. Simon and I have decided ☐
5. Joan explained to me ☐

a. where we're going for our holiday this year – Ghana!
b. he's found that book you were looking for.
c. you could baby-sit for her tonight.
d. how the washing machine works.
e. goodbye. She's going back to Derby tomorrow.

Now match these sentence beginnings with the endings.

6. Will was telling me ☐
7. Brian told me to ask you ☐
8. Anita told me to say ☐
9. Amal persuaded me ☐
10. Nabil explained ☐

f. to go out with her tonight.
g. to me why he hasn't been in class for the last week. His mum has been ill.
h. hi.
i. about his new job. It sounds really good.
j. where you want to meet tomorrow night.

9 Reporting speech (2)

Put the words in brackets in order and make reporting sentences.

1. My wife told ....
   (hello / me / to / say)

2. Jens told ....
   (thanks / me / your / say / to / all / for / help)

3. Clare told ....
   (to / me / to / tell / late / you / tonight / not / be)

4. Stacey told ....
   (tomorrow / to / she'll / late / tell / me / you / be)

5. Ling told ....
   (to / me / luck / test / good / with / say / your / driving)

6. Pascal told ....
   (tonight / to / if / ask / me / could / you / him / you / phone)

7. I saw Diga last week and she ....
   (was / me / move / telling / they're / to / house / going)

10 Talking about crimes

Complete the conversations with the pairs of words in the box.

broke + stole	stolen + have
happen + took	stolen + phoned
steal + put	tried + happen

1. A: I had my bag ....
   B: Oh no! Did you .... much money in it?
   A: Yes – about £150.

2. A: I had my passport ....
   B: Oh no! Have you been to the Embassy and told them about it?
   A: I haven't been there, but I .... them after it happened.

3. A: I had my mobile phone stolen.
   B: Oh no! How did that .... ?
   A: I left it on the table in a café and somebody just .... it.

4. A: Somebody .... to steal my bag.
   B: Oh no! Where did that .... ?
   A: In Holloway Road, near the station.

5. A: Somebody .... into my house and .... some things.
   B: Oh no! Were you insured?
   A: Yes, that's no problem.

6. A: Somebody tried to .... my passport.
   B: Oh no! What happened?
   A: I was on the underground and this person tried to .... their hand in my coat pocket.

1 Key word: *fall*

Find ten sentences with the word fall. Mark the end of each expression using /.

h e f e l l o f f h i s b i k e a n d b r o k e h i s a r m I f e l l
a s l e e p a f t e r l u n c h t h e h a n d l e h a s f a l l e n o f f o n e
o f t h e d r a w e r s I f e l l o v e r i n t h e p a r k t h e p r i c e o f
d i g i t a l c a m e r a s h a s f a l l e n q u i t e a l o t s h e f e l l
d o w n t h e s t a i r s h e r f i r s t t o o t h f e l l o u t
y e s t e r d a y t h e y w e r e g o i n g t o b u i l d a n e w
s c h o o l b u t t h e p l a n s f e l l t h r o u g h I m f a l l i n g
b e h i n d w i t h m y E n g l i s h b e c a u s e I ' v e m i s s e d
s o m a n y c l a s s e s m y s h o e s a r e f a l l i n g a p a r t

Now complete the sentences with ONE word.

1. I fell .... a ladder when I was painting the house and I broke my arm.

2. The baby's fallen .... , so try not to wake him.

3. I need to get a new bike. The one I've got now is falling ....

4. I've had so many problems at home recently I'm falling .... with my studies.

5. Two buttons fell .... my shirt and everyone could see my stomach. It was a bit embarrassing!

6. We were going to take some time off and travel round Europe, but our plans fell ....

2 What a stupid mistake!

Match the sentence beginnings and endings to make five stupid mistakes.

1. I accidentally pressed the accelerator ☐
2. I accidentally clicked 'delete' ☐
3. I accidentally turned the gas up ☐
4. I accidentally added salt ☐
5. I accidentally got on the southbound train ☐

a. instead of sugar.
b. instead of the brake.
c. instead of the northbound one.
d. instead of down.
e. instead of 'save'.

3 Conversation

Complete the conversation with ONE word in each space.

D: Aaagh!

R: Oh, are you all right?

D: Yes, I (1) .... so.

R: Are you sure? That was quite a (2) .... fall.

D: Yes, I don't know what (3) .... I think I just tripped.

R: Yes, you need to be (4) .... Can you stand up all right?

D: Yes, I think so. Ow, ow!

R: (5) .... you should have that arm (6) .... at. It might be broken.

D: No, it'll (7) .... all right. It's probably just bruised.

R: It doesn't look (8) .... it to me. Honestly, I really think you should (9) .... it X-rayed. You don't want to be walking round (10) .... a broken arm.

D: Yes, maybe you're (11) .... It IS quite painful.

R: Shall I get (12) .... a cab to take you to the hospital?

D: Would you (13) .... ?

R: No, of course not. Just sit there for a minute and I'll see if I (14) .... get one. I'll be back in a second.

D: OK. Thanks. I really appreciate it.

Now write the conversation which D has with the doctor at the hospital.

4 Have it done

Match the advice with the reasons.

1. You should have that cut looked at. ☐
2. You should have that tooth looked at. ☐
3. You should have that rash looked at. ☐
4. You should have that ankle X-rayed. ☐

a. It might need a filling or to be taken out.
b. It might need stitches.
c. It might be broken.
d. You might be allergic to something.

Now match the situations with the reasons.

5. I need to get my DVD fixed. ☐
6. I need to get my camera fixed. ☐
7. I need to get my window fixed. ☐
8. I need to get the toilet fixed. ☐

e. It's completely blocked. I can't flush it.
f. Someone threw a brick through it and it's freezing in my room now.
g. The timer's broken, so I can't record programmes while I'm out.
h. The flash doesn't work.

Complete the sentences with ONE word.

i. I had a tooth .... out.
j. Please .... the toilet.
k. Someone threw a brick .... the window.
l. I often .... programmes while I'm ....
m. Did the flash .... ?

Language note: have something done

Notice the structure: subject + *have* + object + past participle. For example:

I've had it X-rayed, but the doctor said it's not broken.
I keep getting headaches, so I'm going to have it checked out.
They had their car stolen yesterday, so they're quite upset.
We're having our house painted at the moment, so I'm afraid you can't stay with us.
Have you had your hair cut?

5 Be careful

Complete the sentences with the words in the box.

bite	burn	drop	hurt
bump	cut	fall	slip

1. It's very hot. Be careful you don't .... yourself!
2. It's very sharp. Be careful you don't .... yourself!
3. The ceiling's quite low here. Be careful you don't .... your head!
4. It's quite fragile. Be careful you don't .... it!
5. It's very heavy. Be careful you don't .... your back.
6. The path goes along the edge of the cliff, so be careful you don't trip and .... ! It's a long way down!
7. He's quite a nervous dog, so be careful he doesn't .... you!
8. The floor's wet. Be careful you don't .... !

Language note: be careful

We often just say *Careful* instead of *Be careful*. For example:
Careful you don't bump your head!
Careful with that vase! It's fragile.

6 Past simple and continuous (1)

Choose the correct form.

1. A: I've hurt my back.
   B: Oh no! How did you do it?
   A: I *was lifting* / *lifted* this heavy box onto the table and it *was happening* / *happened* then.

2. A: Have you heard? Ruth's broken her leg.
   B: You're joking! How did she do it?
   A: She *was playing* / *played* football with her nephew.

3. A: Did you hear Pete crashed his dad's car?
   B: You're joking? How did he do that?
   A: He *was driving* / *drove* too fast as usual and he *was going off* / *went off* the road on a bend.

4. A: How did you hurt your arm?
   B: Oh, I *was falling off* / *fell off* my bike.

5. A: How did you hurt your finger?
   B: Oh, it was stupid. I *was trying* / *tried* to sharpen a pencil with a knife.

6. A: How did you bang your head?
   B: I *was walking* / *walked* into a door.

7 Past simple and continuous (2)

Complete these conversations with the correct form of the verbs.

A: I (1) .... (burn) my hand yesterday.

B: Oh no! How did you do it?

A: I (2) .... (carry) a cup of coffee and someone (3) .... (bump) into me and the coffee (4) .... (go) all over my hand.

C: She (5) .... (break) a bone in her foot when she (6) .... (tidy) up the house.

D: You're joking? What happened?

C: She (7) .... (do) some dusting and she (8) .... (knock) this heavy statue thing off the shelf and it (9) .... (land) on her foot. I'm afraid I (10) .... (laugh) when she (11) .... (tell) me. I shouldn't have, but it was so silly.

8 Apologising

Complete the conversations with the pairs of words in the box.

clumsy + forget	happened + worry
doing + fault	new + purpose
going + let	repaired + silly

1. A: I'm really sorry. I don't know how it ....

   B: Don't .... about it.

2. A: I'm really sorry. I'll pay to get it ....

   B: Don't be .... It wasn't working properly anyway.

3. A: Look where you're .... ! You've knocked my papers all over the floor!

   B: Oh no. I'm sorry. .... me help you pick them up.

4. A: I'm sorry. It just slipped from my hand. I can be so .... sometimes.

   B: .... about it. It was a cheap glass anyway.

5. A: I'm sorry! I don't know what I was .... !

   B: It's OK. It was partly my ....

6. A: I'm afraid you'll have to pay for it. It was brand ....

   B: But it was an accident. I didn't do it on ....

9 Reporting verbs (1)

Match what the speakers are doing with the sentences.

1. blaming someone for something ☐
2. checking something is all right ☐
3. offering to do something ☐
4. making a suggestion ☐
5. complaining about something ☐
6. warning someone about something ☐
7. giving some advice ☐
8. insisting on doing something ☐

a. I'll take you there, if you like.

b. I really think you should go to hospital.

c. He's always leaving his things lying around.

d. Be careful. There's a lot of street crime there.

e. Please let me pay. I won't take no for an answer.

f. It's all your fault.

g. You could try sticking it back together.

h. I just want to make sure everything's arranged.

10 Reporting verbs (2)

Complete the sentences with the verbs in the box.

advised	complained	suggested
blamed	insisted	warned
checked	offered	

1. I .... to the manager about it and he apologised.

2. My doctor strongly .... me to have an operation, so I listened to her and followed her advice.

3. Lots of people .... me about how dangerous Washington is, but I didn't have any problems.

4. I .... trying to ask her parents for the money, but she thought it was a bad idea.

5. It wasn't my fault, but he still .... me for everything going wrong. It was really unfair.

6. I .... all the arrangements before I left, but they still messed up a couple of things.

7. He .... on doing everything, so I just let him!

8. I .... to give him a hand, but he said he was fine on his own.

11 Keywords for writing: *when* and *while*

While shows the action happened over a period of time. We use *while* with the past continuous OR *was/were* + adverbial phrase. For example:

- I broke my leg *while I was living* in France.
- *While I was waiting* for the bus, a man came up and started talking to me.
- I met my husband *while I was on holiday* in Korea.

When is possible in all of these sentences instead of *while*, but we usually prefer *while* in order to emphasise the period of time. When is also used to show an action that happened suddenly or lasted a short time. For example:

- I was driving along *when* suddenly a cat ran into the road.
- *When* I walked into the room, I saw this beautiful woman standing there and I fell in love at first sight.
- *When* I got to the hospital, they did an X-ray.

You cannot replace *when* with *while* in the sentences above because running into a road, walking into a room or getting to a hospital are things which happen very quickly.

There are mistakes in some of these sentences. Underline and correct the mistakes. The first one has been done for you.

1. I was making the dinner <u>while</u> I dropped the frying pan and burnt myself.
   I was making the dinner when I dropped …

2. I hurt my shoulder while I was playing tennis.

3. I was arguing with my girlfriend while I was driving along and I didn't see the red light!

4. While we had dinner, four people phoned me.

5. I had an accident while I was at work.

6. I was lying on the floor playing with my child while the phone rang, and I got up too quickly and hurt my back.

7. My brother was chasing me while I fell over and hurt my knee.

8. While I was in hospital, I met my wife. She was working there as a nurse.

Language note: *during*

We also often use *during* to show a period of time. However, we only use *during* with a noun – and not as part of a clause, as we do with *while*. For example:
I *was sick during the night.* (NOT I was sick ~~while~~ the night.)
It started snowing during the match. (NOT It started snowing ~~during~~ we were playing the match.)
What did you do during the holidays?

12 Writing

Choose the correct words to complete the story.

My friend Rachel and I were chatting (1) ……………… and she was saying how terrible she was at cooking. I (2) ……………… to go round to her house and teach her how to make a couple of dishes.

The (3) ……………… week I went over to her place and we made a couple of really nice dishes. While we were eating, I (4) ……………… smelt something burning. We went into the kitchen and there was a pan on fire. I had (5) ……………… turned up the gas instead of turning it off! We put the fire out quite (6) ……………… , but the kitchen was a mess! I apologised, (7) ……………… Rachel was really annoyed and she didn't speak to me for (8) ……………… !

1. A then	B while	C one day	D when
2. A invited	B said	C asked	D offered
3. A new	B previous	C after	D following
4. A quickly	B suddenly	C hardly	D slowly
5. A hardly	B really	C falsely	D stupidly
6. A quickly	B suddenly	C immediately	D importantly
7. A but	B however	C though	D although
8. A weeks	B month	C long	D now

Now write your own story called *A terrible mistake*. Try and use a variety of time expressions and adverbs.

75

18 Problems

1 Problems (1)

Match the four things with the problems. There are two problems for each thing.

1. a cash card ☐ ☐
2. a bag ☐ ☐
3. a passport ☐ ☐
4. a mini-disc player ☐ ☐

a. I need to get my visa extended. It runs out soon.
b. It's been eaten by the cash machine!
c. It split when I was coming home with the shopping!
d. The batteries are dead.
e. I've forgotten my PIN number!
f. The photo in it was taken ages ago and I look really different now.
g. It's too small. I can't fit everything into it.
h. It's not working properly.

2 Conversation

Complete the conversation with ONE word in each space.

T: Hello. How are you?

A: Great. I've seen lots of interesting things. I'm really enjoying it.

T: Yes, it's a nice place, isn't it?

A: Yes, lovely. So what are you (1) .... today?

T: Oh, I've (2) .... my passport, so I need to go to the Embassy and see if I can get a temporary (3) ....

A: Oh no! Where did you lose it?

T: I'm not sure. The last time I (4) .... having it was in the bank the (5) .... day.

A: Have you been back there to see if anyone's (6) .... it in?

T: Yes, I went there yesterday, but they didn't have it.

A: How annoying!

T: Yes, it's a real (7) .... Anyway, listen. I (8) .... go. The Embassy opens at ten and I want to get there early.

A: Yes, sure. Well, good (9) .... I hope you (10) .... it all out.

T: Yes, thanks.

3 Asking present perfect questions

Make present perfect questions with the verbs in the box. Remember that you will need to use the third form – the past participle – of each verb.

ask	report	take	think

1. A: I left my bag in the classroom earlier, but it's not there any more.
    B: Oh no! ....you .... the security guards in Reception about it?

2. A: I'm finding this English course really difficult.
    B: Really? ....you .... about maybe getting private classes? You could try one-to-one classes, perhaps.

3. A: I've had this cold for about two weeks!
    B: Really? ....you .... anything for it?

4. A: My flat was broken into last night.
    B: Oh no! .... you .... it to the police?

Now make present perfect questions with these verbs.

be	look	phone	speak	tell

5. A: I've lost my purse. You haven't seen it anywhere, have you?
    B: No, I haven't. .... you .... in my coat pocket, though? You borrowed it last night when you were cold.

6. A: I've got a really bad pain in my chest.
    B: Oh no! .... you .... to see anyone about it?

7. A: There's some money missing from my account.
    B: Oh no! .... you .... to your bank about it?

8. A: My boyfriend took my travel card with him to work this morning.
    B: Oh no! .... you .... him and .... him?

Match these answers with the questions above.

1. ☐   2. ☐   3. ☐   4. ☐

5. ☐   6. ☐   7. ☐   8. ☐

a. Yes, I've tried all kinds of things – aspirin, herbs, vitamins – but nothing worked!

b. Yes, I rang my local station as soon as I got home and found out. They were very helpful.

c. Yes, I called them earlier, but they just said it was my fault. They think I spent it!

d. Kind of. I tried to as soon as I realised, but his mobile was turned off. It's so annoying!

e. Oh that's right! I forgot. I'll go and have a look now.

f. Not yet, but I've got an appointment at the hospital tomorrow. I'm really worried about it!

g. That's a good idea. I'll go and ask them if anyone's handed it in to them.

h. No, but it's a good idea. Maybe I'll put an advert in the paper and see if I can find a teacher.

4 | Key word: *sort out*

Translate the expressions into your language.

a   Did you sort out your problem with the passport?

....

b   I still haven't sorted out that problem with my computer.

....

c   I'm trying to sort out my holiday.

....

d   I need to sort out my papers.

....

e   I'm just going to sort out the house.

....

f. I need to sort out my things to take.

....

g   It'll sort itself out.

....

h   Have you sorted out a visa?

....

i   He needs to sort his life out.

....

j. I need to sort out this dirty washing.

....

Now complete the conversations with the expressions.

1. A: I'm so worried about this problem at work I can' sleep properly.

    B: Look, there's nothing you can do about it, is there? Just relax and give it time.
    .... sooner or later.

2. A: He's seeing three different women at the moment – and one of them is married!

    B: He's crazy. ....
    before it gets really bad!

3. A: ....
    It's still crashing all the time.

    B: Oh no! Really? Have you tried taking it to a shop and asking someone there to have a look at it?

4. A: Only three more days till we go on holiday! I can't wait!

    B: ....

    A: Oh, it's OK. You don't need one if you're from an EU country. I just have to take my passport.

5. A: Do you want to go out for a walk?

    B: I'd love to, but I can't, I'm afraid.
    .... Otherwise,
    I won't have any clean clothes to wear tomorrow.

6. A: Hi, Brian. What're you doing here? Shopping?

    B: No, I'm actually looking for cheap flights to Spain.
    ....
    at the moment. I'm thinking of going to Alicante.

7. A: The taxi has arrived. Are you ready to go?

    B: Not yet! ....
    Have you seen my sunglasses and my toothbrush?

    A: Oh no! Haven't you packed yet?

8. A: ....

    B: Yes, I went to the Embassy yesterday and they gave me a temporary replacement.

9. A: Come on. Class has finished. Let's go and have a coffee.

    B: OK, in a minute ....
    and check I've got my pens and everything.

10. A: What're you doing this weekend?

    B: Nothing special. ....
    It needs a good clean. It's a real mess at the moment.

5 Word check (1)

Match the sentence beginnings with the endings.

1. If you really want to get a ticket, you'll have to start queuing the night before they go on ☐

2. There's no money ☐

3. I dropped my walking stick in the street, but this nice young man ☐

4. Oh well, never ☐

5. I felt awful! I was the only Asian person there. Everybody looked at me as if I was an ☐

6. It's nice where I work because everyone is treated ☐

a. alien!

b. left in this machine. Try that one instead.

c. mind. There's nothing you can do about it.

d. sale.

e. fairly. It doesn't matter how old you are or how long you've been there.

f. picked it up for me.

6 Word check (2)

Complete the sentences with the verbs in the box.

catch	join	pay
get	key in	save
introduce	make	

1. The government is going to .... a new law stopping people from smoking in pubs and bars.

2. Can you wait a minute? I just need to .... some money out of the cashpoint.

3. Hi. I'd like to .... this cheque into my account, please.

4. OK. You put your card in here and then you need to .... your PIN number, OK?

5. I'm really worried about it. I don't want to .... the wrong decision.

6. Could you .... my place in the queue for a minute, please? I really need to go to the toilet!

7. I must go. Otherwise, I won't .... the last bus into town.

8. I'm not sure which queue we should .... Which one is moving fastest?

7 Must

Put the words in order and make sentences explaining why you must go.

1. Listen, I must go ....
   (late / I'll / or / be)

2. Listen, I must go ....
   (I'll / flight / or / my / miss)

3. Listen, I must go ....
   (to / my / worry / parents / will / or / start)

4. Listen, I must go. ....
   (me / dinner / tonight / for / sister / is / my / cooking)

5. Listen, I must go. ....
   (I'm / at / some / meeting / of / six / friends / mine)

6. Listen, I must go. ....
   (like / a / on / there's / documentary / watch / TV / I'd / to)

7. Listen, I must go. ....
   (I've / got / an / hour / in / appointment / doctor's / a / half)

8. Listen, I must go. ....
   (to / work / I've / lots / tonight / got / of / do)

8 Machines and technology

Match the sentences with the follow-up comments.

1. I bought a laptop the other day. ☐
2. I bought a Walkman the other day. ☐
3. I bought a dishwasher the other day. ☐
4. I bought a camcorder the other day. ☐
5. I bought a microwave the other day. ☐
6. I bought a washing machine the other day. ☐
7. My wife bought me a DVD the other day. ☐

a. Now I'll be able to listen to music on the train to and from school.

b. Now I'll be able to film my sister's wedding next month.

c. Now I'll be able to work on the train to and from work.

d. Now I won't have to wash up every evening!

e. Now I won't have to go to the launderette any more!

f. Now I won't have to cook every night. I can just buy ready-made meals and heat them up.

g. It's great, but the problem is, I'll have to buy all the films I already have on video again!

9 | Compound nouns

**If you want to dry your hair, you use *a hair dryer*.
What do you need in these situations?**

1. If you want to peel potatoes, you need a
   ....

2. If you want to open a tin, you need
   a ....

3. If you want to sharpen your pencil, you need
   a ....

4. If you want to grate cheese, you need
   a ....

5. If you want to squeeze a lemon, you need a
   ....

6. If you want to remove your nail polish, you need
   ....

7. If you want to open a bottle, you need
   a ....

8. If you want to hang up your coat or shirt in a
   wardrobe, you need a ....

10 | Problems (2)

**Complete the sentences with the words in the
box.**

crashing	out of order	turn up
leaking	turn down	working
making	turn on	

1. The pipe in the bathroom is .... We
   should get someone to come and fix it.

2. It's freezing in here! Can you .... the
   heating .... a bit?

3. We'll have to walk. The lift is ....

4. There's something wrong with the food processor
   It's .... a really funny noise.

5. .... the TV .... The news
   will be on in a minute.

6. It's boiling in here! Can you .... the
   heating .... a bit?

7. There's something wrong with my computer. It keeps
   ....

8. The scanner isn't .... properly. Look – all
   the pictures look really strange.

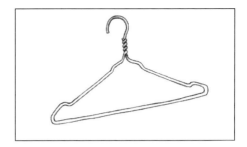

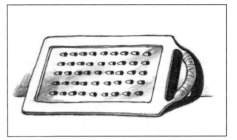

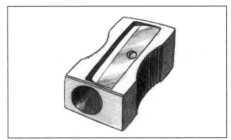

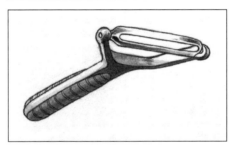

19 Money

1 Borrow and lend

Complete the sentences with the correct form of borrow or lend.

1. Can I .... £5 until tomorrow?

2. Can you .... me £5 until tomorrow?

3. Why don't you talk to your bank about things? Maybe they could .... you some money.

4. Why don't you talk to your bank? Maybe you could .... some money from them.

5. Can I .... your calculator? Thanks.

6. My dad .... me his car for the night – but I crashed it! He's going to kill me!

7. Whatever you do, don't .... any money to Nick. He .... £100 from me last year – and he still hasn't paid me back!

2 Spending time and money

Complete the sentences with the words in the box.

a few pounds	looking	trying
a fortune	studying	watching
all day		

1. He's so lazy. He spends hours every evening sitting at home, ... TV.

2. She goes shopping every weekend. She spends .... on clothes and shoes!

3. A: Hi, Mark. I'm just phoning to see how you are.
   B: Much better, thanks. I spent .... yesterday in bed feeling terrible, but I feel OK today.

4. I don't know where all my money goes. I took £20 out of the cash machine earlier, I spent .... on lunch and now I've got £1.60.

5. I've spent the last two weeks .... for a new place to live – and I still haven't found anywhere!

6. I spent all last weekend .... to fix my car, but It still doesn't work properly.

7. I've got my exams next week. I've spent the last two months just .... I can't wait until they're finished.

3 Conversation

Complete the conversation with ONE word in each space.

B: Have you got time (1) .... a coffee?

T: Yes, OK. Where do you want to go?

B: How (2) .... that place on the corner?

T: Yes, fine. Oh no!

B: What's the (3) .... ?

T: Oh, I've just realised I've (4) .... my wallet at home.

B: Don't worry. It's OK. I'll (5) .... for the coffee.

T: Yes, thanks, but it's not just that. I'm meeting someone at two and I'll have to go (6) .... home and get it. I can't spend the (7) .... day without any money.

B: Well, do you want me to (8) .... you some?

T: Would you (9) .... ?

B: No, of course not. How much do you need? Is €30 enough?

T: That'd be great, if you can.

B: Yes, sure. No problem. I'll just have to go to the (10) .... machine, though. Do you want to meet me in the café? I'll be there in a minute.

T: OK.

B: There you are.

T: Great. That's brilliant. I'll (11) .... you back next week, when I see you.

B: Yes, fine. There's no (12) .... Have you ordered?

T: No, I was waiting for you to get here. I wasn't sure how you like your coffee.

Can you remember where the pauses and the stressed sounds are in this conversation? Mark the pauses // and underline the stressed syllables. For example:

A: Have you got <u>time</u> // for a <u>coffee</u>?
B: Yes, OK. // <u>Where</u> do you <u>want</u> to <u>go</u>?

Compare your ideas about the pauses and stressed sounds with the tapescript in the Coursebook.

4 | Making offers

Match the problems with the offers.

1. I can't get the top off this jar. ☐
2. This bag's really heavy. ☐
3. The cash machine's not working. ☐
4. I'm really hungry. ☐
5. I don't know where to go. ☐
6. I hate walking home in the dark. ☐

a. Do you want me to show you where it is?

b. Do you want me to make you a sandwich?

c. Do you want me to come with you to keep you company?

d. Do you want me to lend you some money?

e. Do you want me to take it?

f. Do you want me to try?

Now write a conversation between YOU and a friend like that in Exercise 3. Use one of the ideas above.

5 | Banks

Complete the sentences with the words in the box.

change	make	open	take out	transfer

1. I'd like to .... my PIN number. I keep forgetting the one I have at the moment.

2. I'd like to .... a new account, please.

3. I'd like to .... a loan. I want to start my own business.

4. I'd like to .... £500 from my savings account to my other account, please.

5. I'd like to .... a complaint. Can I speak to the manager, please?

Now complete these sentences with the words in the box.

cancel	change	close	get	pay

6. I'd like to .... my credit card. I spend too much money on it!

7. I'd like to .... banks. The one I'm with at the moment charges too much interest!

8. I'd like to .... a credit card if I can. I'm sometimes a bit short of money at the end of the month.

9. I'd like to .... this money into my account, please.

10. I'd like to .... my account. I'm moving to another bank!

6 | Money vocabulary

Match the sentence beginnings with the endings.

1. Can I borrow £10? I'll pay ☐
2. He's always buying things for other people. He's really ☐
3. You should get a different credit card. They're charging you ☐
4. You can change money in the post office, but they usually charge you ☐
5. Do you know anywhere I can get a cheque ☐
6. He never buys anything for anyone. He's really ☐
7. If you'd like a credit card, you need to fill in ☐
8. Have you seen Marcus today? I owe ☐

a. mean!

b. £1.50 commission.

c. him £30.

d. 25 per cent interest!

e. you back tomorrow, I promise.

f. cashed?

g. generous.

h. this form first and bring in two proofs of address.

7 | *Charge* and *cost*

Things *cost* money and people or companies *charge* you. For example:

A: *It cost* £40 to have a check-up at the dentist.

B: You're lucky! *My dentist charges* £70 for a check-up.

Complete the sentences with *cost* or *charge*.

1. A: How much did your flight .... ?
   B: £150 with British Airways.

2. A: How much do you .... for private lessons?
   B: £30 an hour.

3. Be careful with that. It .... me a fortune – and I can't afford to replace it.

4. A: How much interest does your bank .... you on your credit card?
   B: About 20 per cent, I think. Why?

5. Our car broke down and it .... us £300 to get it repaired.

6. The bank will change your dollars for you, but they .... four per cent commission.

7. A: Do you .... to have it delivered?
   B: If you live within 25 miles of the shop, then we'll deliver it free of .... If you're outside that area, it will .... £40.

8. It .... us £220 to rent a car for the week. We drove all round the country.

Language note: overcharge, undercharge

If people or companies ask for more money than they should, they *overcharge* you. When people overcharge you, you often complain and ask for your money back. The opposite is when they *undercharge* you. Most people don't complain when this happens!

8 Comparing prices

Complete the sentences with the words in the box.

bar	can	packet	pint
bottle	loaf	pair	tube

1. Bread is much cheaper in my country than it is here. A .... only costs 50p back home.

2. Wine is much cheaper in my country than it is here. A .... only costs two or three pounds back home.

3. Cigarettes are much cheaper in my country than they are here. A .... only costs 80p back home.

4. Coke is much cheaper in my country than it is here. A .... only costs about 30p back home.

5. Toothpaste is much cheaper in my country than it is here. A .... only costs 20p back home.

6. Chocolate is much cheaper in my country than it is here. A .... only costs 10p back home.

7. Jeans are much cheaper in my country than they are here. A .... only costs £15 back home.

8. Beer is much cheaper in my country than it is here. A .... only costs about £1 back home.

Language note: *a can of Coke*

In shops, we buy *cans of Coke* and *bottles of wine*. When we have finished drinking the Coke or the wine, we throw away the empty *Coke cans* and *wine bottles* – or you could recycle them!

9 Key word: *pay*

Complete the conversations with the words in the box.

back	by	for	how	phone
bill	cash	get	into	

1. A: How shall we pay the .... ?
   B: Don't worry about it. I'll get this. It's my treat.
   A: Oh really? Thanks. That's very generous of you.

2. A: Can you lend me some money? I left my wallet at home.
   B: Sorry, but I'm a bit short of money. I've got to pay the .... bill this week.
   A: Oh well, never mind.

3. A: Can you lend me some money? I'll pay you .... tomorrow.
   B: Sorry, but I don't .... paid until the end of the month.

4. A: How much is that?
   B: £85, please. .... are you paying?
   A: I'm not sure. Do I get a discount if I pay .... ?
   B: No, I'm afraid not.
   A: Oh OK. Well, I'll pay .... card, then.

5. I'd like to pay this .... my account, please.

6. A: Wow, I like that hat. How much did you pay .... it?
   B: It was only £12. I got it in the sales.

Complete each sentence from the conversations with ONE word.

a. It's my ....

b. Sorry, but I'm a bit .... of money.

c. I don't get paid .... the end of the month.

d. Do I .... a discount?

e. No, I'm .... not.

f. I got it in the ....

10 Key words for writing: *however, but* and *although*

However, but and *although* are very similar in meaning, but their grammar is different. *But* and *although* connect two parts of the same sentence. *Although* sometimes comes at the start of the sentence. *However* usually starts a new sentence and is followed by a comma. For example:

- You can phone the bank 24 hours a day, *but* it takes them a long time to answer.
- *Although* you can phone the bank 24 hours a day, it takes them a long time to answer.
- You can phone the bank 24 hours a day. *However*, it takes them a long time to answer.

However is more common in written **English. We don't usually use it when speaking or when writing e-mails to friends.**

Join the ideas using the words in brackets.

1. I have written several times to complain. You have still not replied. (however)

    ....

2. I ordered a DVD from your website. I have still not received it. (but)

    ....

3. The DVD player I ordered was finally delivered yesterday. One part is missing. (although)

    ....

4. According to your brochure, the teachers are very experienced. Some of them have never taught before. (however)

    ....

5. I phoned yesterday. You weren't in the office. (but)

    ....

11 Writing

Complete the letter of complaint with the words in the box.

according	complain	enough	ordered
claimed	earliest	help-line	received

Dear Sir / Madam

I am writing to (1) .... about the service I (2) .... from your website www.books4u.co.ge. Over four months ago, I (3) .... a book called *The Joy of Text* (order number xxx3528WAL). You (4) .... that books would be delivered within ten working days, but my order has only just arrived – and it is the wrong book! My book was supposed to be about literature, but the one you sent me is more about biology!

I rang your (5) .... yesterday but I had to wait for over 20 minutes before anyone answered. (6) .... to your website, your staff are friendly and good at their jobs, but the person I spoke to told me that there was nothing she could do. When I told her it was not good (7) .... , she hung up.

To make things worse, I see from my bank statement that you have already taken the money out of my account.

I would like you to either send me the book I originally ordered or return my money at the (8) .... opportunity.

Yours faithfully

Bernard Walker

Language note: *According to*

We often introduce written complaints with the pattern *According to ... , but ... .* For example: *According to your website, you provide a quick delivery service, but I've been waiting over a month for my order to be delivered.*

We can use *However* in a similar way. For example: *According to the brochure, the hotel was supposed to be modern. However, it didn't even have air-conditioning.*

You can also write *According to your newspaper / your publicity / your advert / your assistant / you.* We <u>don't</u> say *According to me.* Instead we write *I told you / informed you that ... , but ... .* If we are giving an opinion, we write *As far as I am concerned, ...*

Now write your own e-mail complaining about something you bought or a service you received.

20 Society

1 Conversation

Complete the conversation with ONE word in each space.

M: What do you do back home?

A: Well, I was working in a car factory, but it closed (1) .... That's why I'm here, really. I got some money when I lost my job and I decided to go travelling for a (2) .... to think about what to do next.

M: And what are you going to do?

A: I still haven't decided. The economy's in a bit of a (3) .... at the moment. There's a lot of (4) .... and people aren't spending much money, so it's going to be difficult to find a new job. I might try to retrain and do something completely different.

M: Have you got any idea what you want to do?

A: Not really. Maybe something with computers. I might try to find a job abroad for a while before I do that. What about your country? Is it easy to find work there?

M: Yes. A few years ago it was quite bad, but the economy's doing quite well at the moment. I think unemployment is about four per cent, so finding a job isn't really a problem. The problem is the (5) .... of living. Prices have gone up a lot over the last few years. Everything is more expensive, so the money you (6) .... goes really quickly.

A: Right.

M: Sometimes I think I should move to somewhere like here. I'm sure people don't get (7) .... very much, but the cost of living is so low and there's a better (8) .... of life. People don't work as hard; life is more relaxed; the food's great; the weather's great; it's just very nice.

A: Yes, maybe, but don't forget that you are on holiday. Maybe it's not like that for the people who live here.

M: No, maybe not.

A: So anyway, how long are you going to stay here?

M: Just (9) .... Friday. I have to get back to work. What about you? How long are you staying?

A: Till I get bored or I (10) .... out of money. I don't have any plans.

2 *How long* questions

Complete the answers with *for*, *since* or *till*.

1. A: How long have you been here?
   B: .... about two weeks now.

2. A: How long are you going to stay here?
   B: .... next Wednesday. Then I'm going back home to Peru.

3. A: How long are you going to stay in Denmark?
   B: Just .... a couple of days.

4. A: How long have you been working here?
   B: .... I left university, so .... about eight years now.

5. A: How long are you going to study for?
   B: .... 2011. It takes a long time to become a doctor, you know!

6. A: How long have you been playing the guitar?
   B: Oh, ... a long time – .... I was about six.

3 Your country

Complete the second sentence in each pair so that it has the opposite meaning.

1. Lots of new factories are opening up.
   Lots of factories are ....

2. The economy is in a bit of a mess.
   The economy is .... very
   ....

3. There's a lot of unemployment.
   Unemployment is quite ....

4. The cost of living is really low.
   The cost of living is quite ....

5. The currency is very weak.
   The currency is very ....

6. The quality of life is great.
   The quality of life isn't very ....

Which sentences are true for your country at the moment?

4 What society is like

Match the sentences with the summary statements.

1. Everything is very cheap, especially basic things like rent and food. ☐
2. There are 15,000 rupiah to the dollar at the moment. ☐
3. Prices haven't gone up much this year. ☐
4. It's a very relaxed place. People take their time. No-one is in a rush. It's lovely. ☐
5. Unemployment is very low and inflation is low too. Lots of new factories are opening up and new companies are starting. ☐

a. Our currency is very weak.
b. The cost of living is very low.
c. The economy is doing very well.
d. The pace of life is very slow.
e. Inflation is very low.

Now match these sentences with the summary statements.

6. It's very easy to find work at the moment. ☐
7. Most people don't earn very much. ☐
8. The weather isn't very nice; the people can be quite cold and unfriendly, and there's quite a lot of crime. Most people work really long hours as well. ☐
9. I don't have to pay much of the money I earn to the government. ☐
10. The average wage is really high. Most people live in really nice places. The roads are excellent and so are the schools and the hospitals. ☐

f. The average wage is only about $150 a month.
g. Tax is quite low – about twelve per cent.
h. Unemployment is very low.
i. The standard of living is very high.
j. The quality of life isn't very good.

Language note: *in a rush*

If the pace of life is quite slow, no-one is *in a rush* / *in a hurry*. If you are late for something, you can say *I've got to go. I'm in a rush.* If you need more time to do something, you can say *Don't rush me.* If someone suddenly becomes really ill or if they have an accident, they're *rushed to hospital*.

5 Time expressions

Put the words in order and make time expressions.

1. last / over / the / years / few

   ....

2. or / over / four / last / months / the / three

   ....

3. the / last / of / weeks / over / couple

   ....

4. over / three / days / last / two / the / or

   ....

5. was / since / kid / I / a

   ....

6. I / was / 14 / since / or / 13

   ....

7. I / university / graduated / since / from

   ....

8. started / here / I / since / working

   ....

6 Describing changes

Chose the correct form.

1. Unemployment *is going down* / *has gone down* a lot over the last few months.
2. Inflation *is going up* / *has gone up* over the last month.
3. Crime *is getting* / *has got* worse and worse at the moment.
4. The weather *is getting* / *has got* hotter and hotter over the last 20 or 30 years.
5. My English *is improving* / *has improved* a lot over the last few weeks.
6. Racism *is getting* / *has got* worse at the moment.
7. *He's getting* / *He has got* really well paid at the moment.
8. *She's looking* / *She's looked* for a new car at the moment.
9. *I'm* / *I've been* really busy at work at the moment.
10. *I'm* / *I've been* really busy at school over the last few weeks. I've got my exams in two weeks' time.

7 News stories

Complete the sentences with the words in the box.

charity	trade unions
going on strike	vegetarian
the environment	

1. I'll have to drive to work tomorrow because I heard on the news that all the bus drivers are ....

2. Hi, I'm collecting money for an old people's .... Would you like to make a donation?

3. This government lets big businesses pollute the rivers and the air. It doesn't care about .... It's awful!

4. I've heard so many horrible things on TV about how they kill animals I've decided to become a ....

5. If you ask me, ... have too much power! They're always going on strike and asking for more money!

Now complete these sentences with the words in the box.

designer clothes	retire
housework	the economy
partner	

6. The government is doing OK, I think. They said on the news that .... is doing so well that they won't need to borrow any money from the World Bank this year!

7. They said on the news earlier that men are doing more .... than ever before! They obviously haven't met my dad! He still thinks it's women's work!

8. She makes good money, but she has to look smart at work, so she spends a lot on expensive ....

9. He said he's bringing his .... to the party tonight. I'm really looking forward to meeting her!

10. My parents told me that they want to move to the south of France when they finally .... I can't believe it!

8 Talking about society

Match the sentence beginnings with the endings.

1. Nurses are going on strike next month. They want shorter ☐

2. Teachers are on strike at the moment. They want a bigger ☐

3. My father lost his job last year. The factory he was working in ☐

4. I lost my job last year. My boss thought I wasn't ☐

5. I didn't vote in the last election because all the parties ☐

6. I voted for the Green Party in the last election. They've promised to do more for ☐

a. were the same!

b. pay rise than the one they've been offered.

c. working hours.

d. good enough! I was really angry about it!

e. the environment.

f. closed down

9 Talking about people you know

Complete the sentences with the pairs of words in the box.

age + grey	memory + forgets
deaf + hear	problems + trouble
eyes + glasses	short + tall
immature + grow up	wheelchair + frail

1. Her .... are still really good. She only wears .... for reading.

2. He's really .... for his age. He needs to .... !

3. She's completely .... now. She can't .... a thing.

4. She's quite .... for her age. She's only 1 metre 50 ....

5. He's losing his .... He .... what he's doing all the time.

6. He's having .... at school. He's always getting into ....

7. She has to use a .... She's too .... to walk.

8. He's starting to look his .... now. He's gone .... very suddenly. He used to look so young!

Language note: *look your age*

When someone *doesn't look their age*, it means they look younger than they actually are. When someone *starts to look their age*, they look – and are – old! You can also *feel your age*, especially when you can't do the things you used to be able to do. People often say *you're only as old as you feel*. It means you can be 50, but inside you feel as if you are 30!

10 Used to (1)

Complete the story with *always* or *never*.

I'm 87 now and things have changed a lot since I was young. When I was growing up, people were much more polite. Men (1) .... used to hold doors open for women and people would offer their seats on buses to old people, but nobody does that any more. Young people (2) .... used to use bad language on the street or argue with their parents, but lots of teenagers nowadays do that kind of thing. One thing that is better now, though, is life for women. Seventy or eighty years ago, young women (3) .... used to be allowed out without someone to watch them. When boys and girls went out together, parents (4) .... used to send a family friend to make sure nothing strange happened. Girls (5) .... used to wear make-up either. It wasn't allowed. All that has changed. Parents were stricter then, too. My dad (6) .... used to ask me where I was going and he (7) .... used to tell me what time he wanted me home. I (8) .... used to lie to him or break his rules. I was too scared! It's probably nicer being young nowadays because parents are more liberal. One nice thing about my dad, though, was that he (9) .... used to hit us. Oh, and also he (10) .... used to help us with our homework. That was nice.

Complete each expression from the story with ONE word.

a. .... doors open for women

b. .... their seats to old people

c. use bad ....

d. .... make-up

e. .... his rules

Now write a paragraph about how life in your country has changed. Try to use *always used to* and *never used to*.

11 Used to (2)

Match the sentence beginnings with the endings.

1. I never used to smoke till a few years ago, ☐
2. I used to drive really fast, ☐
3. I never used to be interested in foreign languages, ☐
4. I used to live in a lovely big house in the centre of town ☐
5. I used to have really long hair and wear a nose ring, ☐
6. I used to sleep until midday on Saturday mornings, ☐
7. I used to go out a lot more than I do now, ☐
8. I used to play basketball for a local team, ☐

a. but when I lost my job, I couldn't afford the rent any more, so I moved.

b. but my new girlfriend is Swiss. She speaks French and Italian – but not much English!

c. but I realised I needed to change the way I looked if I wanted to get a job.

d. but I got a job which starts at six in the morning, so I need to go to bed earlier now!

e. but I had an accident a few years ago and I've slowed down since then.

f. but I was really stressed out at work. That's why I began.

g. but I broke my leg a few years ago and had to stop.

h. but now I get up early and go for a run instead. It's nice to do more exercise.

Answer Key

Introduction

1 What is a collocation?

1. d.   2. a.   3. e.   4. b.   5. c.   6. h.   7. j.   8. f.   9. g.   10. i.

2 Making the most of your self-study time

Students' own translations.

3 Grammatical terms

1. b.   2. c.   3. d.   4. g.   5. f.   6. a.   7. h.   8. e.

1 Where are you from?

1 Starting conversations

1. b.   2. c.   3. a.   4. d.   5. g.   6. h.   7. e.   8. f.

2 Conversation

1. smoke   2. stop   3. again   4. exactly   5. coast   6. love
7. going   8. home   9. take   10. reason

3 Where and whereabouts

1. Blackpool   2. Carlisle   3. Anglesey   4. Birmingham
5. Inverness   6. Hastings   7. Gloucester   8. Dumfries

4 Whereabouts exactly is it?

1. D   2. B   3. E   4. A   5. C   6. F

5 I'm not from here originally

1. refugee   2. escape   3. degree   4. support   5. brought up
6. closed down   7. unemployment   8. degree   9. graduate
10. immigrant   11. holiday   12. miss   13. share

6 Moving

1. work, company   2. job, unemployment   3. escape, safe
4. family, old   5. sea, coast   6. study, university   7. get away
from, know   8. place, houses

7 There's / there are ...

1. There are   2. There's   3. There's   4. there's   5. there are
6. There's   7. there are   8. There are

8 There's a ...

1. take-away   2. park   3. mall   4. bookshop   5. factory
6. café   7. cinema   8. supermarket

a. way   b. take   c. can't   d. get   e. where   f. open

9 Miss and lose

1. lost   2. miss   3. lost   4. lost   5. missed   6. missed   7. lost
8. missed   9. miss   10. miss

10 Key words for writing: so and because

1. because   2. so   3. so   4. because   5. because

11 Writing e-mails: changing address

1. A   2. D   3. C   4. A   5. D   6. A   7. B   8. A

We often start e-mails:
Sorry I haven't written to you recently, but I've been busy …
Just a quick e-mail to tell you …

We often end e-mails:
See you soon.
Love OR All the best

2 Likes and dislikes

1 Verb forms

1. go   2. take   3. break   4. leave   5. read   6. meet   7. choose
8. eat   9. forget   10. fall   11. know   12. drink   13. see
14. give   15. hear   16. buy

2 Conversation

1. it   2. ask   3. thinking   4. trying   5. else   6. kind   7. Lots
8. him   9. same   10. prefer   11. heard   12. lend

3 Do you like ... ?

1. They're OK, I suppose.   2. Yes, I love it.   3. No, I hate it.
4. Yes, it's OK.   5. Yes, I love him.   6. I've never heard of her.
7. No, not really.   8. I've never heard of them.

4 What kind ... ?

1. d.   2. a.   3. f.   4. e.   5. b.   6. c.

5 Verbs

1. chat   2. argue   3. invite   4. share   5. spend   6. support
7. ring   8. join

6 How do you know each other?

1. c., d.   2. a., f.   3. e., h.   4. b., g.

7 Key word: go

1. bed, swimming   2. holiday, own, a friend   3. round to, for
4. to get   5. ahead   6. the toilet   7. your exam, well

8 Too

1. near   2. far   3. hot   4. hot   5. early   6. late   7. old
8. young   9. good   10. late

9 Too fast / too much

1. weight, eats   2. can't understand, talks   3. makes, does
4. get to sleep, were playing   5. a stomach-ache, ate
6. annoys, talks   7. a car crash, drives   8. a heart attack, works

10 Pen friends

1. A   2. A   3. B   4. C   5. A   6. D   7. C   8. B

11 Would you like ... ? / Do you like ... ?

1. Would you like   2. Do you like   3. Would you like   4. Do
you like   5. Would you like   6. Do you like   7. Do you like
8. Would you like

3 Have you got ... ?

1 Have you got a / any ... ?

1. cloth, spilt   2. plasters, cut   3. pen, write down
4. screwdriver, unscrew   5. correction fluid, made
6. dictionary, means

1. b.   2. a.   3. c.   4. e.   5. f.   6. d.

2 One / some

1. some   2. some   3. one, one   4. one   5. some   6. one

3 Things in the house

shelves C   kitchen table E   fridge D   wardrobe F   top drawer H   desk A   cupboard G   bottom drawer I   sink B

4 Prepositions of place

1. in, in   2. in, under   3. on, in   4. on / under, in   5. in, in
6. in   7. in, in   8. on, in

5 Conversation

1. just   2. have   3. better   4. on   5. them / any   6. found / got
7. were   8. mine

6 Oh no!

1. spilt   2. lost   3. left   4. forgotten   5. cut   6. torn
7. dropped

7 Everyday things

1. dustpan and brush   2. stapler   3. envelope   4. corkscrew
5. needle   6. rubber   7. torch   8. knife

8 I'm thinking of ...

1. e.   2. f.   3. a.   4. b.   5. d.   6. c.

9 Explaining decisions

1. use   2. burn   3. falling   4. repair   5. breaking down
6. park   7. get on with   8. contact

10 Questions and answers

1. e.   2. f.   3. b.   4. g.   5. a.   6. d.   7. c.

11 Which one? That one!

1. the one   2. the ones   3. The first one   4. These ones
5. The ones   6. These ones   7. The one   8. the one

12 Key words for writing: but and though

1. but   2. but   3. though   4. though   5. though   6. but

13 Writing e-mails

1. thank you   2. send   3. love   4. congratulations   5. but
6. though   7. E-mail   8. best

14 Starting letters and e-mails

1. looking for   2. studying   3. doing   4. moved   5. thanks
6. sorry

4 Times and dates

1 Do you know what the time is?

1. It's a quarter past eight.
2. It's half (past) four.
3. It's ten to seven.
4. It's twenty to nine.
5. It's just gone eleven.
6. It's almost half (past) one.
7. It's almost a quarter to five.
8. It's just gone a quarter past two.
9. It's almost twenty past five.

2 Conversation

1. going   2. might   3. no   4. does   5. later   6. own   7. want
8. shall   9. could   10. about   11. sounds   12. time   13. gone

3 What are you doing at the weekend? – present continuous or might

1. 'm / am meeting   2. might go   3. are coming   4. might come   5. might go   6. 'm / am going   7. 're / are having
8. 'm / am going   9. is coming, 's / is arriving   10. might have

The other common verb-noun collocations are: going to an Italian place, depends on the weather, do some shopping, bought me a ticket, got any plans.

4 Making arrangements

Conversation 1: c. a. b. e. d.
Conversation 2: b. e. d. a. c.
Conversation 3: d. c. a. e. b.

5 Verbs that go with time

1. takes   2. have   3. arrange   4. have   5. spent   6. 's

6 I'll always remember it

1. B   2. A   3. B   4. C   5. A   6. A   7. D   8. D   9. C   10. C

7 Special days

1. my birthday   2. Independence Day   3. Valentine's Day
4. wedding anniversary   5. public holiday

8 I hope

1. pass   2. get   3. lose   4. win   5. likes   6. isn't   7. doesn't rain   8. isn't delayed

9 Time expressions

1. minute   2. sometime   3. other   4. tomorrow   5. in
6. week

10 What are they going to do?

1. b.   2. e.   3. d.   4. a.   5. c.

11 Key word: look

1. look   2. looking   3. look   4. a look   5. look   6. looking
7. a look   8. look

5 Buying things

1 Clothes

1. trainers   2. swimsuit   3. bracelet   4. T-shirt
5. sunglasses   6. boots   7. coat   8. suit and tie

2 Describing people

2. the / that short guy with the dark hair
3. the / that guy with the dark glasses and the long coat
4. the / that thin woman with the blond hair
5. the / that fat guy with the tight jeans standing over there
6. the / that woman with the long brown hair at the table by the window
7. the / that tall man with the glasses talking to the black woman

3 Conversation

1. Are they new?   2. They really suit you.   3. to begin with
4. They've got a sale on   5. I just couldn't resist them   6. I can imagine   7. reduced from 65   8. Whereabouts exactly   9. it's about halfway down   10. thanks for telling me

4 I got it in the sale

1. half-price   2. reduced from   3. get one free   4. special offer, off   5. staff discount   6. ten per cent   7. sell-by-date

5 I need to do some housework

1. washing   2. shopping   3. ironing   4. hoovering   5. tidying up   6. repairs

6 Enough

2. I left my last job because the money wasn't good <u>enough</u>.

3. I'd like to get a ticket for the concert, but I don't have <u>enough</u> money.

4. This doesn't taste right. It's not sweet <u>enough</u>.

5. I didn't finish my homework. I didn't have <u>enough</u> time.

6. The public transport here is terrible! There aren't <u>enough</u> buses or trains!

7. I'm afraid I can't play tennis today. I don't feel well <u>enough</u>.

8. I don't really like this kind of music. It's not fast <u>enough</u>.

7 I can't! It's too big.

1. g.   2. h.   3. a.   4. b.   5. f.   6. c.   7. e.   8. d.

8 Not enough

1. tall   2. big   3. good   4. clever   5. brave   6. rich   7. fit   8. long

9 Asking negative questions

1. e   2. a   3. d   4. c   5. b   6. f

10 Key words for writing: *also, too* and *as well*

1. I study very hard, but I like playing golf too.

2. I like reading and writing, and I also do photography.

3. I go out a lot, but I like staying in and reading as well.

4. I have a degree in computer science and I also have a Master's in business management.

5. There are lots of cafés and pubs near where I live and there's a big cinema as well.

6. The university has a large library and a sports centre, and it also has a modern conference centre.

2. As well as liking reading and writing, I do photography.

3. As well as going out a lot, I like staying in and reading.

4. As well as having a degree in computer science, I have a Master's in business management.

5. As well as there being lots of cafés and pubs near where I live, there's a big cinema.

6. As well as having a large library and a sports centre, the university has a modern conference centre.

11 Writing – personal statements

1. want   2. interested   3. taught myself   4. free time   5. first prize   6. too   7. especially   8. specialist courses

6 How are you?

1 I'm a bit fed up

1. my English   2. my mum and dad   3. the weather   4. my job   5. the weather   6. the flat we're renting   7. these classes   8. my English   9. my mum and dad   10. my job   11. the flat we're renting   12. these classes

2 Conversation (1)

f. d. b. e. a. h. c. g.

i. sure   j. nice   k. very   l. bit   m. all

3 Questions and answers

1. bug, sick   2. bad, days   3. painkillers, better   4. hospital, fine   5. weak, easy

4 Infinitives of purpose

1. b.   2. g.   3. a.   4. h.   5. f.   6. e.   7. c.   8. d.

5 Conversation (2)

1. actually   2. upset   3. awful   4. do   5. kind   6. take   7. sounds   8. see

6 I had a really late night

1. b.   2. a.   3. f.   4. c.   5. e.   6. d.   7. k.   8. g.   9. l.   10. h.   11. i.   12. j.

7 Talking about sleeping

1. fell asleep   2. had nightmares   3. went to bed   4. stay awake   5. overslept, wake up   6. asleep

8 Can't / couldn't

1. d.   2. g.   3. c.   4. f.   5. h.   6. e.   7. a.   8. b.

9 What about you?

1. I didn't, actually. I got woken up three or four times by the noise outside.

2. Oh, I'm OK, thanks.

3. I'm meeting a friend, actually. I haven't seen her for ages.

4. I went to Berlin with my wife, actually. We only got back home at twelve last night.

5. Oh, I haven't really been doing much, actually. Things have been quite quiet.

a. well   b. long   c. ages   d. in   e. back   f. Things

10 Good news

1. married   2. exams   3. promoted   4. birthday   5. visa   6. holiday   7. place   8. best friend

1. g.   2. b.   3. a.   4. f.   5. c.   6. e.   7. d.   8. h

7 School and studying

1 Your academic career

1. graduated   2. Master's   3. degree   4. job   5. secondary school   6. university   7. leaves   8. do   9. primary schools   10. left   11. do   12. go   13. Master's   14. PhD

2 Conversation

1. B   2. D   3. A   4. C   5. A   6. C   7. D   8. C

3 Going to

1. b.   2. a.   3. d.   4. c.   5. g.   6. h.   7. f.   8. e.

4 *Going to* or *might*

1. are (you) going to do, 'm / am going to start   2. 's / is going to fail, might pass   3. are (you) going to do, 'm / am going to study, might take, 'm / am (definitely) not going to go   4. 'm / am going to stay, 'm / am going to see, might want

a. offered   b. away   c. behind   d. catch   e. spare

5 Studying at university

a. rewrite   b. apply to   c. pay back   d. find   e. retake   f. give

1. lecture, fell   2. exam, taking   3. university, dropped out   4. term, term   5. essay, started

6 Could you just ...?

1. c.   2. a.   3. b.   4. e.   5. d.   6. i.   7. g.   8. f.   9. h.   10. j.

7 Key words for writing: *even though* and *although*

1. I got the job even though I didn't have any experience.
2. I got a job in Japan even though I didn't speak any Japanese.
3. Even though I didn't study, I passed my exam.
4. Even though I handed in my application form late, they gave me an interview.
5. They're going to move to Italy even though they don't speak Italian and they haven't got any work there.

In sentences 1, 4 and 6 you can only use *although*. In 2, 3 and 5 you can use both.

8 Writing

1. shame   2. advice   3. quit   4. find   5. with   6. experience
7. at   8. qualifications

8 | Work and jobs

1 Questions and answers

1. b.   2. d.   3. a.   4. e.   5. c.   6. i.   7. h.   8. f.   9. j.   10. g.

2 Conversation

1. Are you working or studying or what?
2. what do you do?
3. Do you enjoy it?
4. Do you have to work weekends?
5. And do you get much holiday?
6. do you have to travel very far to work?
7. what about you?

3 Do you enjoy your job?

1. have to   2. don't have to   3. don't have to   4. have to
5. don't have to   6. don't have to

4 I have to ...

1. c.   2. e.   3. b.   4. a.   5. f.   6. d.

5 Jobs

1. designer   2. instructor   3. manager   4. driver   5. guard

6 Compound nouns

1. football   2. ticket   3. book   4. alarm   5. car

a. car crash   b. fire alarm   c. football shirt   d. ticket machine
e. textbook   f. car mechanic   g. bookshelf   h. football stadium

7 My job

1. sacked   2. flexible   3. times   4. earn   5. take   6. days off
7. easy   8. little   9. college   10. leave   11. get   12. over
13. hours   14. afternoons   15. published   16. novel   17. Apart
from   18. long   19. stressful   20. all   21. dying
22. paperwork   23. equipment   24. well-paid

8 Present perfect

1. Have (you) been to (our country before?)
2. Have (you) travelled (round Europe much?)
3. Have (you) seen (any good films recently?)
4. Have (you) heard (the new Bobby Zamora CD?)
5. Have (you) had (much experience of this kind of work?)
6. Have (you) taken (anything for it?)
7. Have (you) played (this game before?)
8. Have (you) ever eaten (snake?)

1. c.   2. a.   3. f.   4. b.   5. d.   6. g.   7. h.   8. e.
i. about   j. like   k. rubbish   l. easy   m. quick

9 Vocabulary: getting a job

1. thing, office work   2. interested, the job   3. an application
form, details   4. fill in, company   5. an interview, brilliant
6. the interview, hope   7. offer, start   8. the job, celebrate

9 | Eating out

1 What was the restaurant like?

1. spicy   2. portions   3. choice   4. full   5. food, waiters
6. empty

2 There's a nice place ...

1. seafood   2. quite a lot   3. Greek Street   4. me   5. work
6. quite cheap   7. a buffet for lunch   8. outside

3 Conversation

1. a   2. get   3. mind   4. corner   5. for   6. like   7. else   8. in
9. like   10. lots   11. sure   12. anything   13. Shall   14. up

4 Refusing food and drink

1. I'm really full.
2. I don't drink.
3. I'm on a diet.
4. I mustn't have any more.
5. I don't really like anything spicy.
6. I don't really like anything sweet.
7. I've just had one.
8. I won't be able to sleep.
9. I couldn't eat another thing.

5 *Some* and *any*

1. some, some   2. Any, any   3. any   4. any, some   5. any, some,
any   6. some   7. any, some   8. some, any, any

6 Irregular past simple

1. bent, tore   2. fell, felt   3. broke, had, cost   4. went, ate, felt
5. wrote, put, sent, tore, saw, told

7 Restaurant vocabulary

1. e.   2. a.   3. h.   4. b.   5. c.   6. g.   7. d.   8. f.

8 Food: ways of cooking

chopped G   grilled B   boiled D   roasted H   fried J
mashed I   squeezed C   steamed A   toasted F   sliced E

1. Toasted, chopped   2. Steamed, roasted   3. Grilled, mashed
4. boiled   5. squeezed   6. sliced

9 Key words for writing: *then* and *so*

1. so   2. and then   3. so   4. Then   5. so   6. Then, and then
7. so   8. and then

10 Writing: recipes

1. First   2. While   3. and then   4. so   5. After   6. Then
7. until   8. Finally

10 | Family

1 Questions we ask about families

1. h.   2. c.   3. g.   4. b.   5. e.   6. a.   7. d.   8. f.

2 Married

1. engaged, the big day   2. marry   3. get married   4. extended
5. reception   6. separated, divorce   7. immediate   8. registry
office

3 Conversation

1. are you doing 2. 'm / am going round 3. does she live
4. does she do 5. works 6. older 7. older 8. more
organised 9. have been married 10. will be

4 Describing what people are like

1. She's very funny.
2. He's a bit shy.
3. He's really nice.
4. He's very generous.
5. She's a bit quiet.
6. He's very honest.
7. She's very relaxed.
8. She's really fit.

1. f. 2. g. 3. b. 4. h. 5. a. 6. d. 7. e. 8. c.

5 Comparatives

1. older 2. more hard-working 3. quieter 4. taller
5. younger 6. more relaxed 7. fitter 8. lazier 9. more open
10. more serious

a. find b. all c. goes d. work e. career

6 My family

1. C 2. A 3. D 4. A 5. A 6. C 7. C 8. A 9. C 10. D

7 Collocations

1. d. 2. b. 3. f. 4. e. 5. a. 6. c.

8 Expressions with *friend*

1. just good friends 2. a friend of a friend 3. is it OK if I
bring a friend 4. my friends from university 5. made any
friends 6. my friend from Peru 7. a few close friends

9 Died of / died in

1. war 2. overdose 3. cancer 4. sleep, age 5. AIDS

10 The internet and computers

1. download 2. on-line 3. check, sent, answer, receive
4. damage, crashed 5. go, member

11 Getting around

1 Around town

1. subway 2. crossing 3. monument 4. lights, church
5. junction, signs 6. bridge 7. roundabout 8. stadium

2 Verbs for giving directions

1. d. 2. a. 3. b. 4. c. 5. e. 6. g. 7. h. 8. f.

3 Conversation

1. know 2. way 3. idea 4. round 5. area 6. again 7. place
8. somewhere 9. sure 10. Follow 11. straight 12. until
13. there 14. get 15. hope

4 You're best … -ing

1. taking the bus 2. going by coach 3. taking the tube
4. getting a taxi 5. getting the train 6. e-mailing 7. going to
8. talking to

5 Indirect questions

1. Could you tell me where the toilet is?
2. Could you tell me what time the class starts?
3. Could you tell me what stop I need to get off at?
4. Could you tell me how much the tickets are?
5. Could you tell me if there are any places left on the course?

6. Could you tell me how long the course lasts?
7. Could you tell me if the coursebooks are included in the fees?
8. Could you tell me who I need to speak to about the course?

6 Can / could

1. can't 2. couldn't 3. could 4. can't 5. can 6. couldn't
7. could 8. can / could 9. can't

7 Travel compound nouns

1. traffic jam 2. travel card 3. roadworks 4. main road
5. car parks 6. transport system 7. rush hour 8. car
insurance 9. return ticket 10. side street 11. transport
system 12. main road 13. side street 14. car insurance
15. car parks 16. roadworks 17. traffic jam 18. travel card

8 Travel conversations

Conversation 1: c. a. b. d.
Conversation 2: d. c. b. a.
Conversation 3: c. a. d. b.
Conversation 4: b. a. d. c.
Conversation 5: b. e. c. a. d. g. f.

9 Key words for writing: *when* and *until*

1. until 2. When 3. when 4. until 5. when 6. until
7. when 8. when 9. until 10. until

10 Writing – giving directions

1. Take 2. come out of 3. cost 4. keep going 5. along
6. See you

1. come out of 2. keep going 3. along 4. take 5. cost
6. see you

12 Free time

1 When was the last time?

1. h. 2. b. 3. d. 4. e. 5. f. 6. a. 7. c. 8. g.

2 Conversation

1. do 2. see 3. good 4. lot 5. once 6. hardly 7. kind /
sort 8. mainly / mostly 9. not 10. time

3 Adding information

2. I stayed in and watched a / this programme, *Holly Oak,* about Ireland.
3. I'm reading a / this book, *Upside Down,* about Australia.
4. I went to a / this restaurant, Lalibella, in Tufnell Park.
5. I went to see a / this new film, *Down With Love,* with my boyfriend.
6. I went to see a / this exhibition, *The New Modernists,* at the Tate Gallery.

4 Do you do that a lot?

1. go 2. use 3. see 4. wear 5. cook 6. work 7. take
8. leave

1. b. 2. a. 3. c. 4. e. 5. f. 6. h. 7. g. 8. d.

5 Who do you support?

1. e. 2. a. 3. f. 4. d. 5. g. 6. b. 7. c.

6 Cup or league?

1. C 2. L 3. L 4. C 5. L 6. C 7. C 8. L 9. L 10. L
11. L 12. C

7 Superlatives (1)

1. fittest   2. oldest   3. laziest   4. tallest   5. nicest   6. easiest
7. most interesting   8. youngest   9. most relaxed   10. most
beautiful

8 Superlatives (2)

1. e.   2. a.   3. f.   4. b.   5. g.   6. c.   7. h.   8. d.

9 Photos

1. taking   2. press   3. the zoom   4. closer   5. further   6. fit
7. smile   8. take   9. light   10. Cheese

10 Present simple for talking about the future

1. leaves   2. gets into   3. finish   4. start   5. is   6. kicks off
7. lasts

11 Know how to

1. how to develop   2. how to drive   3. how to ski   4. how to
serve   5. how to set up   6. how to boil   7. how to play
8. how to get

13 Places to stay

1 Using vocabulary: places to stay

1. c.   2. f.   3. b.   4. a.   5. e.   6. d.
g. pitch   h. electricity   i. stove   j. room   k. site   l. twisted
m. screamed

2 Booking a room in a hotel

1. take   2. booking   3. paying   4. number   5. expiry   6. on
7. booked   8. forward   9. confirmation / proof   10. with
11. wait   12. been

3 First conditionals

1. 'll give, want   2. 'll go, like   3. 'll take, like   4. 'll make, like
5. 'll do, have   6. 'll come, have to   7. 'll help, find   8. will be,
don't buy   9. will (just) get worse, don't do   10. will sell out,
don't get

4 Hardly

1. hardly ever   2. hardly eaten   3. hardly anyone   4. hardly
breathe   5. Hardly anything   6. hardly any   7. hardly done
8. hardly hear

5 Almost everyone / hardly anyone

1. every   2. all   3. any   4. all   5. any   6. no   7. always

6 Key word: stay

stayed up late, stay in all day, stays cool, stayed in bed all
morning, stay for dinner, how long are you staying?, stay till the
end, where are you staying?, stay the night, it won't stay on,
what time does that bar stay open till?, everything just stays
the same

1 stayed in bed all morning   2 stay till the end
3. stayed up late   4. stay in all day   5. stay the night
6. stays cool   7. it won't stay on   8. everything just stays the
same   9. stay for dinner   10. Where are you staying?
11. What time does that bar stay open till?   12. How long are
you staying?

7 As long as

1. f.   2. a.   3. b.   4. e.   5. g.   6. h.   7. d.   8. c.

8 Keywords for writing: because of and despite

1. because of   2. despite   3. because of   4. despite   5. despite
6. because of   7. despite   8. because of

9 Writing

1. B   2. D   3. A   4. A   5. C   6. B   7. D   8. B   9. A   10. C

14 What was it like?

1 Good times, bad times

1. e.   2. f.   3. d.   4. b.   5. c.   6. a.   7. l.   8. i.   9. j.   10. g.
11. k.   12. h.
great: 2, 3, 6, 9, 10 and 11
terrible: 1, 4, 5, 7, 8 and 12

2 Conversation

1. for   2. mine   3. think   4. Most   5. couple   6. like   7. such
8. about   9. much   10. spent   11. ever   12. went / was

3 Talking about your experiences

Conversation 1: c, e, a, d, b
Conversation 2: 1. time   2. day   3. actually   4. think
5. tasted   6. nice
Conversation 3: 1. ever   2. for   3. doing   4. studying
5. speak   6. going   7. there   8. first   9. Whereabouts
10. travel

4 Answering Have you ever ... ? questions

1. No, never, but I'd love to.
2. No, never, but I've always wanted to.
3. No, never, but it's supposed to be brilliant.
4. No, never, but I've never really wanted to.
5. Yes, I have, actually, but I didn't really like it.
6. Yes, I have, actually, but I'm not sure I'd do it again.
7. Yes, I have, actually – quite a few times.
8. Yes, I have, actually. It was a couple of years ago now.

5 He's always complaining!

1. g., i.   2. d., h.   3. c., e.   4. a., j.   5. b., f.

6 Expressions with have

a. I had this horrible virus.   b. We had a great time.   c. I had
an argument.   d. Do you want to go and have something to
eat?   e. I had a terrible time.   f. Have you had anything to eat?
g. I had an appointment.   h. I haven't had anything to eat.
i. I had to have the whole week off.   j. I had a big breakfast.

1. we had a great time   2. I had a terrible time   3. Have you
had anything to eat?, I haven't had anything to eat.   4. I had this
horrible virus, I had to have the whole week off   5. Do you
want to go and have something to eat?   6. I had a big
breakfast   7. I had an argument   8. I had an appointment

7 Asking what things are like.

1. c.   2. e.   3. d.   4. b.   5. a.   6. g.   7. f.

i. very   j. get   k. much   l. cramped

8 Asking longer questions

2. (What was that) hotel you stayed in in Naples (like?)
3. (What's that) guy you play tennis with (like?)
4. (What's that) company your brother works for (like?)
5. What's the area you've moved to like?
6. What was that party (you went to) at Colin's (house) like?
7. What was that play you went to see last week like?
8. What was that Chinese restaurant you and your boyfriend
   went to last week like?

93

15 What's on?

1 Films

1. f.   2. c.   3. e.   4. a.   5. b.   6. d.

2 Conversation

1. planned   2. seeing   3. supposed   4. last   5. else   6. really
7. do   8. about   9. review   10. on   11. where   12. shall
13. something   14. there   15. 'll

3 Questions about films and programmes

1. Who's it by?   2. Who's in it?   3. Where's it on?
4. What's on?   5. What time's it on?   6. Who's it by?
7. What time's it on?   8. What's it about?   9. What's it about?
10. Where's it on?   11. What's on?   12. Who's in it?

4 Famous people

1. presents   2. plays   3. made   4. paints   5. writes
6. invented   7. leads   8. developed

5 Meeting a famous person

1. A   2. C   3. C   4. A   5. B   6. B   7. A   8. D

6 TV and video

1. turn the TV up   2. turn over, record   3. set the video
4. rewind   5. turn the TV down   6. turn the TV on, turned it
off

7 What does it say in the TV guide?

1. bad (*dull* means '*boring*')   2. good (horror films should be
scary!)   3. good (*fascinating* means '*very interesting*')   4. good
5. good (dramas should be moving!)   6. bad   7. bad   8. good

The key words are: *dull, (genuinely) scary, fascinating, brilliant,
moving, dreadful, (very) over-rated* and *enjoyable*.

8 The passive or active?

1. was delayed   2. was cancelled   3. cancel, was stolen   4. be
picked up   5. happened   6. was caught   7. caught   8. got
woken up   9. stars   10. was directed

9 Key words for writing: *if, what, how, where* and *when*

1. how   2. if   3. what time   4. what   5. if   6. if   7. how much
8. how many   9. how long   10. which   11. if   12. when

10 Writing letters of enquiry

1. further information   2. to your website   3. doesn't say
4. wanted to know   5. worried   6. find out   7. clarify   8. look
forward to

16 Telephoning

1 Key word: *phone*

1. d.   2. a.   3. e.   4. b.   5. c.   6. i.   7. f.   8. j.   9. g.   10. h.
k. call   l. on   m. on   n. in   o. book

2 Conversation

1. there   2. name   3. same   4. told   5. say   6. help   7. few
8. able   9. spare   10. time   11. give   12. thank

3 Answering the phone

1. 'll   2. 'll   3. 's   4. might   5. might, might   6. 's, might

4 Prepositions

1. in   2. on   3. out   4. off   5. in   6. out   7. off   8. between
9. on   10. at

5 Summarising expressions

1. embarrassing   2. annoying   3. funny   4. horrible
1. b   2. a   3. d   4. c
5. frightening   6. amazing   7. depressing   8. disgusting
5. f.   6. e.   7. h.   8. g

6 -ed / -ing adjectives

1. interested   2. frightening   3. annoyed   4. frightened
5. bored   6. excited   7. boring   8. exciting   9. annoying
10. interesting

7 Texting

1. ala   2. oic   3. xlnt   4. ltns   5. atm   6. afda   7. wan2
8. b4n

9. gr8 news   10. cu l8r   11. it's ezi   12. thx 4 the info
13. ruok?   14. myob   15. cu 2nite   16. it's up 2 u   17. cu
2moro   18. can u do it asap?

8 Reporting speech (1)

1. c.   2. e.   3. b.   4. a.   5. d.   6. i.   7. j.   8. h.   9. f.   10. g.

9 Reporting speech (2)

1. (My wife told) me to say hello.
2. (Jens told) me to say thanks for all your help.
3. (Clare told) me to tell you not to be late tonight.
4. (Stacey told) me to tell you she'll be late tomorrow.
5. (Ling told) me to say good luck with your driving test.
6. (Pascal told) me to ask you if you could phone him tonight.
7. (I saw Diga last week and she) was telling me they're going
to move house next year.

10 Talking about crimes

1. stolen, have   2. stolen, phoned   3. happen, took   4. tried,
happen   5. broke, stole   6. steal, put

17 Accidents

1 Key word: *fall*

He fell off his bike and broke his arm.
I fell asleep after lunch.
The handle has fallen off one of the drawers.
I fell over in the park.
The price of digital cameras has fallen quite a lot.
She fell down the stairs.
Her first tooth fell out yesterday.
They were going to build a new school but the plans fell
through.
I'm falling behind with my English because I've missed so many
classes.
My shoes are falling apart.

1. off   2. asleep   3. apart   4. behind   5. off   6. through

2 What a stupid mistake!

1. b.   2. e.   3. d.   4. a.   5. c.

3 Conversation

1. think   2. nasty / bad   3. happened   4. careful   5. Maybe /
Perhaps   6. looked   7. be   8. like   9. have / get   10. with
11. right   12. you   13. mind   14. can

4 Have it done

1. b.   2. a.   3. d.   4. c.   5. g.   6. h.   7. f.   8. e.
i. taken   j. flush   k. through   l. record, out   m. work

5 Be careful

1. burn 2. cut 3. bump 4. drop 5. hurt 6. fall 7. bite
8. slip

6 Past simple and continuous (1)

1. was lifting, happened 2. was playing 3. was driving, went
off 4. fell off 5. was trying 6. walked

7 Past simple and continuous (2)

1. burnt / burned 2. was carrying 3. bumped 4. went
5. broke 6. was tidying 7. was doing 8. knocked 9. landed
10. laughed 11. told

8 Apologising

1. happened, worry 2. repaired, silly 3. going, Let 4. clumsy,
Forget 5. doing, fault 6. new, purpose

9 Reporting verbs (1)

1. f. 2. h. 3. a. 4. g. 5. c. 6. d. 7. b. 8. e.

10 Reporting verbs (2)

1. complained 2. advised 3. warned 4. suggested 5. blamed
6. checked 7. insisted 8 offered

11 Keywords for writing: *when* and *while*

2. correct

3. correct

5. While we were having dinner, …

4. correct

6. I was lying on the floor playing with my child when
the phone rang …

7. My brother was chasing me when I fell over …

8. correct

12 Writing

1. C 2. D 3. D 4. B 5. D 6. A 7. A 8. A

18 Problems

1 Problems (1)

1. b., e. 2. c., g. 3. a., f. 4. d., h.

2 Conversation

1. doing 2. lost 3. one / replacement 4. remember
5. other 6. handed / given 7. pain 8. must 9. luck 10. sort

3 Asking present perfect questions

1. Have (you) asked 2. Have (you) thought 3. Have (you)
taken 4. Have (you) reported 5. Have (you) looked 6. Have
(you) been 7. Have (you) spoken 8. Have (you) phoned, told
1. g. 2. h. 3. a. 4. b. 5. e. 6. f. 7. c. 8. d.

4 Key word: *sort out*

1. It'll sort itself out
2. He needs to sort his life out
3. I still haven't sorted out that problem with my computer
4. Have you sorted out a visa?
5. I need to sort out this dirty washing
6. I'm trying to sort out my holiday
7. I need to sort out my things to take
8. Did you sort out your problem with the passport?
9. I need to sort out my papers
10. I'm just going to sort out the house

5 Word check (1)

1. d. 2. b. 3. f. 4. c. 5. a. 6. e.

6 Word check (2)

1. introduce 2. get 3. pay 4. key in 5. make 6. save
7. catch 8. join

7 Must

1. (Listen, I must go) or I'll be late.
2. (Listen, I must go) or I'll miss my flight.
3. (Listen, I must go) or my parents will start to worry.
4. (Listen, I must go.) My sister is cooking dinner for me
tonight.
5. (Listen, I must go.) I'm meeting some friends of mine at six.
6. (Listen, I must go.) There's a documentary on TV I'd like to
watch. OR There's a documentary I'd like to watch on TV.
7. (Listen, I must go.) I've got a doctor's appointment in half an
hour.
8. (Listen, I must go.) I've got lots of work to do tonight.

8 Machines and technology

1. c. 2. a. 3. d. 4. b. 5. f. 6. e. 7. g.

9 Compound nouns

1. potato peeler 2. tin opener 3. pencil sharpener
4. cheese grater 5. lemon squeezer 6. nail-polish remover
7. bottle opener 8. coat hanger

10 Problems (2)

1. leaking 2. turn (the heating) up 3. out of order
4. making 5. Turn (the TV) on 6. turn (the heating) down
7. crashing 8. working

19 Money

1 *Borrow* and *lend*

1. borrow 2. lend 3. lend 4. borrow 5. borrow 6. lent
7. lend, borrowed

2 Spending time and money

1. watching 2. a fortune 3. all day 4. a few pounds
5. looking 6. trying 7. studying

3 Conversation

1. for 2. about 3. matter 4. left 5. pay 6. back 7. whole
8. lend 9. mind 10. cash 11. pay 12. hurry / rush

4 Making offers

1. f. 2. e. 3. d. 4. b. 5. a. 6. c.

5 Banks

1. change 2. open 3. take out 4. transfer 5. make
6. cancel 7. change 8. get 9. pay 10. close

6 Money vocabulary

1. e. 2. g. 3. d. 4. b. 5. f. 6. a. 7. h. 8. c.

7 *Charge* and *cost*

1. cost 2. charge 3. cost 4. charge 5. cost 6. charge
7. charge, charge, cost 8. cost

8 Comparing prices

1. loaf 2. bottle 3. packet 4. can 5. tube 6. bar 7. pair
8. pint

9 Key word: *pay*

1. bill   2. phone   3. back, get   4. How, cash, by   5. into   6. for
a. treat   b. short   c. until   d. get   e. afraid   f. sales

10 Key words for writing: *however, but* and *although*

1. I have written several times to complain. However, you have still not replied.
2. I ordered a DVD from your website, but I have still not received it.
3. Although the DVD player I ordered was finally delivered yesterday, one part is missing. OR The DVD player I ordered was finally delivered yesterday, although one part is missing.
4. According to your brochure, the teachers are very experienced. However, some of them have never taught before.
5. I phoned yesterday, but you weren't in the office.

11 Writing

1. complain   2. received   3. ordered   4. claimed   5. help-line
6. According   7. enough   8. earliest

20 Society

1 Conversation

1. down   2. while   3. mess   4. unemployment   5. cost
6. earn   7. paid   8. quality   9. till   10. run

2 *How long* questions

1. For   2. Till   3. for   4. Since, for   5. Till   6. for, since

3 Your country

1. closing down   2. doing (very) well   3. low   4. high
5. strong   6. good

4 What society is like

1. b.   2. a.   3. e.   4. d.   5. c.   6. h.   7. f.   8. j.   9. g.   10. i.

5 Time expressions

1. over the last few years
2. over the last three or four months
3. over the last couple of weeks
4. over the last two or three days
5. since I was a kid
6. since I was 13 or 14
7. since I graduated from university
8. since I started working here

6 Describing changes

1. has gone down   2. has gone up   3. is getting   4. has got
5. has improved   6. is getting   7. He's getting   8. She's looking
9. I'm   10. I've been

7 News stories

1. going on strike   2. charity   3. the environment
4. vegetarian   5. trade unions   6. the economy   7. housework
8. designer clothes   9. partner   10. retire

8 Talking about society

1. c.   2. b.   3. f.   4. d.   5. a.   6. e.

9 Talking about people you know

1. eyes, glasses   2. immature, grow up   3. deaf, hear   4. short, tall   5. memory, forgets   6. problems, trouble   7. wheelchair, frail   8. age, grey

10 Used to (1)

1. always   2. never   3. never   4. always   5. never   6. always
7. always   8. never   9. never   10. always

a. hold   b. offer   c. language   d. wear   e. break

11 Used to (2)

1. f.   2. e.   3. b.   4. a.   5. c.   6. h.   7. d.   8. g.